The Crazy Wisdom of
GANESH BABA

"For those unlucky enough to have missed him in the flesh, this text offers the next best thing: a distillation of Ganesh Baba's most fundamental teachings, his unique and prophetic synthesis of East and West, science and spirituality, madness and method. Through personal narrative Eve portrays the fun and frustrations of learning from a crazy guru whose profound and mischievous ways blew our minds to infinity!"

ROXANNE KAMAYANI GUPTA, PH.D., AUTHOR OF
A YOGA OF INDIAN CLASSICAL DANCE

"Add this endearing, wise, and well-named 'Trickster' to the list of great teachers. His message was clear: mind can only point to the Truth, to find it you have to live it truly and fully for yourself!"

ALICE O. HOWELL, AUTHOR OF *THE HEAVENS DECLARE*

"In this loving and insightful spiritual memoir, author Eve Baumohl Neuhaus introduces us to her larger-than-life, iconoclastic spiritual teacher and his all-encompassing Cycle of Synthesis. True to his name, Ganesh Baba, he bursts through the barriers of any preconceived Western notions of a guru. She offers a simple yet profound spiritual practice based on his teachings that would delight her teacher and draws together contemporary Western spiritual seekers with the ancient wisdom of the East."

HEATHER MENDEL, AUTHOR OF
DANCING IN THE FOOTSTEPS OF EVE AND *TOWARDS FREEDOM*

Ganesha Mantra

गजाननम् भूत गणादि सेवितम्

कपित्य्यजम्बू फल चारु भक्षणम्

उमा सुतम् रोक विनाशकारकम्

नमामि विघ्नेश्वर पाद पंकजम्

The Crazy Wisdom of
GANESH BABA

Psychedelic Sadhana, Kriya Yoga, Kundalini, and the Cosmic Energy in Man

EVE BAUMOHL NEUHAUS

Inner Traditions
Rochester, Vermont • Toronto, Canada

Inner Traditions
One Park Street
Rochester, Vermont 05767
www.InnerTraditions.com

Text paper is SFI certified

Library of Congress Cataloging-in-Publication Data

Neuhaus, Eve Baumohl.
  The crazy wisdom of Ganesh Baba : psychedelic Sadhana, Kriya yoga, Kundalini,
and the cosmic energy in man / Eve Baumohl Neuhaus.
      p. cm.
  Includes index.
  ISBN 978-1-59477-265-8 (pbk.)
  1. Baba, Ganesh. 2. Yoga, Kriya. I. Title.
  BL1238.56.K74N48 2010
  294.5092—dc22
  [B]
                                                              2009052972

Printed and bound in the United States by Lake Book Manufacturing
The text paper is 100% SFI certified. The Sustainable Forestry
Initiative® program promotes sustainable forest management.

10   9   8   7   6   5   4   3   2   1

Text design by Jon Desautels
Text layout by Virginia Scott Bowman
This book was typeset in Garamond Premier Pro, Agenda, and Caflisch with
Arepo, Agenda, and Gill Sans as display typefaces

To send correspondence to the author of this book, mail a first-class letter to the
author c/o Inner Traditions • Bear & Company, One Park Street, Rochester, VT
05767, and we will forward the communication.

*To my beloved Satguru, Shri Mahant Swami Ganeshanand,
and to Yogacharya a Tripura Charan Devesharma before him,
and to all my teachers, with deepest gratitude.*

Baba in France (photo by Michèle Cruzel)

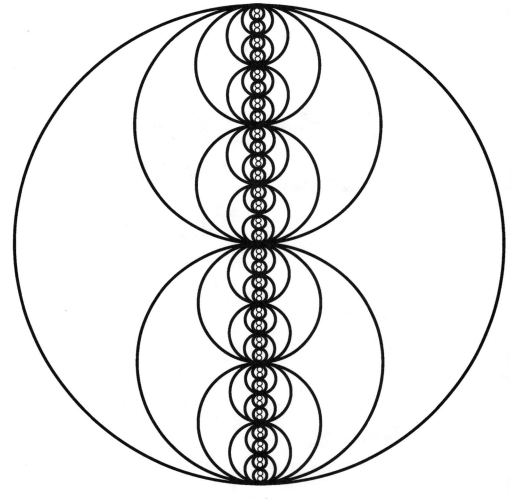

To infinity

CONTENTS

Ganesh Baba and Ehud Sperling, New York City, winter 1981.
Photo by Ira Cohen.

PUBLISHER'S PREFACE

In a word, outrageous! That was my experience of Ganesh Baba or GB as he was fond of being called, the brown Santa Claus from planet India. He walked into my office one morning and was living with me that evening. Carrying only a small bag with a change of clothing, this wandering renunciate was living the high life in New York City, with literally only the clothes on his back. Baba and I became good friends, roommates, and fellow travelers, and I had some of the most extraordinary experiences of my life in his presence.

"Baba please don't bring every single person you meet in the street up to our apartment," I would say to him. He would pay me no mind. Baba's love was indiscriminate, and he was as likely to engage a homeless person as a sophisticated scientist. One day I returned from work at the publishing house to discover a young lady had just moved into my home. Baba had met her earlier that day on Broadway—just two blocks from my home—had heard her story, and decided to bring her home with him. I couldn't believe it! However, my concern and trepidation was soon turned into affection and appreciation for the lovely human being that Baba had brought into our lives. She stayed with us for a few days, receiving Baba's teaching, and then was off on her journey. Two days later a famous poet arrived with his entourage. He'd come straight from the airport to meet the psychedelic guru Ganesh Baba. He walked in and touched Baba's feet as is the tradition in North India when you greet a senior and distinguished individual. It is a sign of humility and respect for the teacher. Before the poet lifted his head, Baba's hand came sweeping down across his face, slapping him senseless and throwing him to the ground. I was quite taken aback and wondered what would transpire, seeing the shock and outrage in the eyes of my other guests. No sooner had the poet regained his composure than did he start recounting a series of transgressions and sins for which he was asking Baba's forgiveness. Baba laughed, demanded a joint, and the party began.

Baba at work.

This was one of many festive occasions I enjoyed with Baba. People were always wanting to throw parties for him in New York, and one night we were invited to a large loft in Soho for a celebration in honor of the Shri Mahant Ganesh Baba. Earlier that day a friend of Baba's had come by the apartment with some psilocybin mushrooms. Before leaving for the party, Baba painstakingly ground the sacred mushrooms in a mortar and pestle and mixed them into a lassi, which he insisted I share with him. As we entered the loft that evening the mushrooms started taking effect and within a few moments Baba was lost to me in a crowd of a few hundred. As the doors of perception were opening, in marched a troop of naked women, Brazilian samba dancers, decorated only with feathers and moving to the sound of conga drums. Bare breasts and glistening buttocks sinuously glided past the audience and on to the stage that had been set up for the occasion. At the head of this procession was none other than Ganesh Baba. I saw him on the stage and could see he was lost in an ecstatic trance; his eyes pointed up into his skull and the hands and legs of his 90-year-old body were swaying in abandon. I was terrified! At any moment he could fall off the stage and the evening would quickly turn from ecstasy to trials and tribulations. I ran up to the stage and grabbed Baba who, as he came back to earth, turned to me and said, "Joint." He was very fond of cannabis—as are all of his Naga brethren, saints, and sadhus—in a tradition that dates back to the beginning of time.

Baba defied labels and categories: swami, guru, father, brother, teacher, saint, Naga baba, yogi, tantric, scientist, linguist, psychedelic hipster, Kriya yogi, and devotee of the Divine Mother. None of these terms alone, nor a collection of them together, can in any way summarize or indicate the extraordinary man that you'll be reading about in this book. The few months that he spent living with me in New York City count among the most important of my life. He lifted my spirits, he tore away illusion, he exhibited compassion, his extraordinary intellect had a command of both religion and science.

Baba went horseback riding with Winston Churchill, studied physics with Einstein. He and his tantric buddies brought down the presidency of Richard M. Nixon. He was raised from the dead as a child and had developed the unified theory of physics, the mathematics of which he was working on with a scientist at Berkeley. Ganesh Baba considered the hippies that came to India in the 1960s to be the finest people on earth. His use of ethnogens was just an adjunct in his practice of spiritualization through Sadhana. He was a traditional swami and guru in the Kriya Yoga lineage as well as a Shri Mahant in one of the major Naga

Acharyas. During the time we spent together my publishing life was turned upside down, and I spent most evenings well into the morning hours talking with Baba on subjects both esoteric and mundane. Like a whirlwind he lifted me up and threw me into a marriage with India that continues to the present day in the person of my wife, Vatsala, a Tamil from Madurai.

Baba was an embodiment of his teaching and the tradition of crazy wisdom that dates back to the Rishi's of ancient India. Even at 90 years of age his energy was inexhaustible, based as it was on a constant practice of Kriya yogic breathing. If anybody was fading around Baba, a hug while he was breathing deeply would instantly energize them. Unattached unencumbered, liberated and free to act as the spirit moved him, to be with Baba was to be transformed. I hope that the pages that follow can in some small way give you a taste of the extraordinary, outrageous, and indomitable spirit of Ganesh Baba.

EHUD C. SPERLING

ACKNOWLEDGMENTS

Om gam Ganapataye namah
Om namah Shivaya
Om namah Saraswataya
Om namah Lakshmaya
[I respect the presence of these deities within me]

I am ever grateful for the power of Ganesh to open doors and break down barriers. I thank Shiva for bringing creation out of destruction over and over again; and I thank Saraswati (Wisdom) and Lakshmi (Luck) for gracing my house with their presence once and always.

Deep thanks to Roxanne Gupta for bringing Baba to me and me to India, to Jayant Gupta for his all blessings and teachings, and to Corinne Vandewalle and Christian Pilastre for being with me on this journey so long. Thank you all for your abiding friendship, wisdom, and extraordinary support of this work in many forms.

Thanks to my husband, Tom Neuhaus, for working so hard to provide me the time and space to write the book, and for his ever-open heart and mind; and thanks to my children, Elisa, Brendan, James, Juliet, and Linnea, for putting up with such eccentricity all their lives.

Thanks, too, to Ehud Sperling, for not giving up on this project for thirty years. We did it!

Thanks to Hari Meyers for firing my enthusiasm with his own; to David Stuart Ryan for the 1966 synopsis of *Sadhana;* to Tony Donohoe for sharing the early days of the journey with me; to Brendan Donohoe for his computer savvy; to Judy Brown for coming so early and staying so late; to Peter Meyer for taking care of Baba in Oakland; to Keith Lowenstein for all those copies; to Dan Kraak for his straight back and delightful smile; to Dr. Lokesh Chandra and Baba Rampuri for broadening my understanding of the context in which Ganesh Baba wrote the manuscript; to all the French Crea family for loving Baba; to Shri Devi, Deniz Tekiner, and Micaela Toledo for giving me just the help I needed at the time; to Ira Landgarten for providing Baba's voice to accompany me as I worked; to my Thursday group and many other friends for listening as I processed and reprocessed this material; to David Michael Kennedy for the inspirational photos of Baba; to Robert and Melanie Sachs for their wisdom, friendship, and support through the writing; to the teachers at Pacifica Graduate Institute and CIIS for extending my understanding of the material; to Heather Mendel for friendship and encouragement; to Mark Dyczkowki and Eckhart Tolle for moving me forward when I was stuck; to Alice O. Howell for her blessings and wisdom.

Thanks, finally, to Mindy Branstetter and the team at Inner Traditions for their gracious help in fulfilling my promise to Ganesh Baba.

I am in your debt.

> *Divine Mother*
> *You, whose body and soul are my own,*
> *Whose substance creates reality,*
> *Illuminate also my heart*
> *That it, too, may do your work.*

Introduction
SADHANA

Om namo ganeshaya!
Mantra used at the beginning
of a project praising Lord Ganesh
and asking his blessing

Swami Ganeshanand
Divine Life Society
Darjeeling, West Bengal

SYNOPSIS:

Amen!

Ameen!

Hum!

We must lose no time in realizing the gravity of our
present predicament as a specific species geared to free will.
Though our free will may be not entirely or absolutely free it
is also not fettered by any blind, lack-law or lack-love fate.
We must realize the gravity of our failure, in our specific
property (the gyro-compass of free will), spirituality; and each

1

of us must make it our bounden responsibility to realize our respective shares in the lapse of our species and seek remedy to our individual lapses, which by and large add up to the totality of the general lapse of our species in regard to its most specific property, for example, spirituality.

The next revolution is going to be a spiritual one, and it will have to touch off a chain reaction of personal revolutions leading to total revolution, individual changes leading to a social change. Each of us is responsible for the real revolution in the offing, the revolution of modern man, the modern matter-mad spirit-oblivious man, trying to turn his face toward the spirit, steering an even course between matter and spirit, a harmonious combination of both as complementary aspects of the one Integral Reality. None can conscientiously disclaim his or her responsibility in which one has to kill nothing but his or her own vices, including lack of spirit or failure of faith. If you are not doing so you are hindering humanity in its general progress.

The Principles of Scientific Spiritualization amplified by Sri Ganesh
Original author: Yogacharya Srimat Tripura Charan Devasharma
Containing the Principles of Cosmic Action, or Kriya

This is the beginning of Ganesh Baba's synopsis of his manuscript *Sadhana,* or Spiritual Practice, which is in turn his translation and updating of the manuscript, also called *Sadhana,* of his guru, Tripura. It isn't uncommon in India for a teacher to give a student such a document to rewrite; in fact, it's a teaching strategy. *The Crazy Wisdom of*

Prayer

Oh, the Glorious, the ever Beautiful, Pure Superble Pure; the Supreme Being; the eternal Existence; the Cosmic Life — the Universal Self!

Though Thou art One Undifferentiated Ultimate Universal Unity, — the Ut-Integral, still Thou art manifest as the Many as in the Theire Play Cosmic — Leela, as they say, — in all the names and forms!

Please Do grant us the aspiration an the ability to serve and understand Thee! May the service to Thee be verily the vow of our life. Please do grant us the vision to view Thee in every form.

Thee have become 'we'. Please do transform our 'I'-ness into Thee, 'Thy'-ness. Thou have become our beloved sons, daughters, grand children and many other loving relation and have kept us tied in a sweet bond

From one of Ganesh Baba's many undated notebooks

Ganesh Baba is the granddaughter of Tripura's *Sadhana,* translated and updated again. It also includes two stories, the story of my guru, Ganesh Baba, and another about the process of writing the book, an attempt to capture the evolution of the practice.

My copy of a copy of the late 1960s manuscript, which I used as the basis of the book, is not finished. It's a draft. Baba gave copies of it, along with his two even-less-finished manuscripts and piles of essays, to a number of his followers. Polish this up, bring it up to date, he said, and publish it. When he assigned *Sadhana* to me, he even supplied the publisher.

A book like this can never really be finished. The material memories, three book-length manuscripts, piles of loose papers, notebooks, audio- and videotapes, and countless hours of practice will never fit into a book; it's too generative. It changes as fast as it's written down, and just when you think you're on top of it, it vanishes. Ink fixes words and images in time; the real substance of what someone like Ganesh Baba passes on can't be held down—it's too subtle—it slips out between the warp of language and weft of thought and escapes.

Nonetheless, here is my attempt at capturing a little of the magic of Shri Mahant Swami Ganeshanand Saraswati and Giri, outrageously High Hipster, Rainbow Head, Psychedelic Swami, Naga baba, Kriya yogi, scientist, scholar, and British Indian gentleman, and to convey the essence of his teachings.

It's an almost unbearable honor to continue in the tradition.

1

CREA SADHANA

Once and Always

It's said that when the student is ready, the teacher will come.

The day Ganesh Baba came, I was not ready. In fact, I was late. It was a Sunday afternoon in the fall of 1979. I had two small children and a ramshackle country house to look after, and I was done looking for teachers.

So, waiting in line to meet the teacher whom my friends Jayant and Roxanne Gupta had brought from India, autumn sun slanting across the tables of the little café called the New Delhi in Geneva, New York, I was completely unprepared for the sense of recognition I felt when our eyes met. I never imagined that his hand in mine would feel as familiar as my father's, or that his face would be as recognizable as my own in the mirror. Once I met Baba, I knew I had always known him.

"Ah cha," he said, smiling and wagging his head in satisfaction. "We meet again!" It was true.

Two days later, Roxanne and Jayant brought Baba to visit our farmhouse in Ovid.

Because he was staying in upstate New York only a few days before flying to California for eye surgery, and it might be my only chance to see him, I was eager to spend as much time with Baba as possible. He, in turn, tried to teach me as much as he could in the time we had.

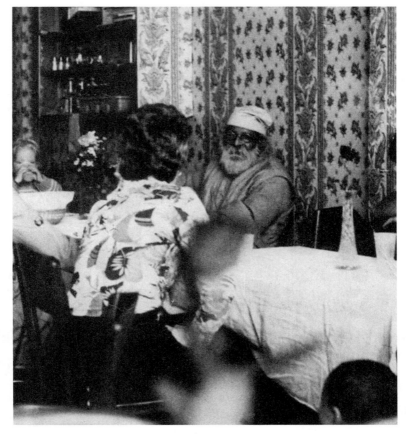

Ganesh Baba at the New Delhi the day I met him

The images and understandings that he passed on to me over that three-day period still serve as the lens through which I see life.

As it turned out, I spent three years rather than three days in close contact with Ganesh Baba. About halfway through that time, he decided that we should work on his manuscripts. Baba traveled with three bags containing all his possessions: an old suitcase holding his kurtas* and trousers, all orange, and a few books; a shoulder bag for his snuff, the insulin and syringes he used to keep his diabetes in check, sugarless candies, a worn address book, and his current reading; and a

---

*[A kurta is a long, loose-fitting collarless shirt of Indian origin. —*Ed.*]

A rendering of how Ganesh Baba looked the first time he came to our house in Ovid (illustration by Brendan Donohoe)

small case of papers containing his correspondence, three book-length manuscripts, and a stack of essays and notes. He chose the manuscript called *Crea Sadhana* for our work together. *Sadhana,* which translates roughly to "spiritual practice," is his updated version of his own guru Shri Tripura Charan Devasharma's book, also titled *Sadhana.* I felt flattered and excited to be part of continuing the tradition.

The process was not so simple, however. Nothing is simple when dealing with the embodiment of Lord Ganesh, who is both the god of obstacles and the god of their removal.

In that period, Baba would come to stay at our house for a few days at a time. We'd sit together at the typewriter in the study, blankets folded on his bed behind us, his single suitcase open, the smell of his snuff everywhere. Laboriously, I'd rework a page typed by an Indian typist long ago, often a third carbon copy on crumbling legal-size vellum, or perhaps a page from a manuscript retyped by Corinne Vandewalle or another student more recently in Kathmandhu or Benaras. The work was slow, not only because I am a terrible typist—I had to borrow a typewriter to do the work—but because Baba's system of doing the work involved stopping so frequently to change the newly typed material. He was, as usual, ahead of his time; a word processor would have been the right tool for the job, not a manual typewriter. As it was, each revision required pulling the paper out of the typewriter, whiting out the section to be corrected, waiting for the correction fluid to dry, reinserting the paper in the roller, and getting it aligned properly before the section could be retyped.

Asking students to type and retype his written work was one of Baba's teaching methods. I don't know how many of us there are around the world who did at least some of this work, but there could well be dozens of versions of his papers tucked away in files or wrapped in cloth

Shri Tripura Charan Devasharma
(photo courtesy of Anil, his son)

Lahiri Mahasaya

and lying on a shelf or under an altar, as my copies of his work did for so many years.

Each writing session began with a cup of hot chai, and then, more often than not, a joint or two. Learning to do focused work in an altered state was part of the training.

Ganesh Baba, formally Shri Mahant Swami Ganeshananda Saraswati, or Giri, was a member of two very distinct lineages of Indian teaching. The first is the Lahiri line of Kriya Yoga, a distinguished group of teachers who taught householders* a streamlined version of yoga until then only practiced by monks and renunciates. Beginning with the venerated Lahiri Mahasaya, the Kriya yogis modernized yoga, emphasizing its scientific nature. Ganesh Baba shares his descent in this line with Paramahansa Yogananda, who brought Kriya Yoga to the West in the 1920s.

---

*Householders are just regular people, as opposed to monks or renunciates.

The second line to which Ganesh Baba is heir is more ancient and less respectable, at least in many circles. Baba was Shri Mahant, or headman, of the Dasnami order of the Anand Akhara, a Naga sect. His guru was Suraj Giri Maharaj. Nagas are the ash-covered, often-naked babas, who wander through India emulating the god Shiva, wild-eyed and intense from smoking charas, a potent mixture of cannabis resin and tobacco.

By the time I met him, Ganesh Baba was well into the *sanyasin* (renunciate) stage of his life. He'd left behind his family and work, and even his name and his history, long before coming to America. The stories he told us about his past were shared with us as teaching stories, and, like all good stories, were not meant to be taken literally. Depending on the purpose and setting of the telling, the versions we students heard varied significantly. We never knew his real age or background before his renunciation, causing some contention among us at times. After Baba's death in 1987, Western disciples went to India and uncovered a history not completely at odds with the stories he told, but not the same either.

As the Indian sage says, "Tree is like a saint or guru. Tree provides fruits and nourishment, shade and protection from inclement weather, dry branches for fuel, and the leaves for thatching material for the hut. If you dig the roots, the tree will die."

Intoxicated Shiva

In the story Baba told me, he was the oldest son of a middle-class Bengali family, born at the height of the British Raj. When he was a very young child, he nearly died of cholera. At the age of four years, four months, and four days old, his parents brought him, on his deathbed, to the great Lahiri Mahasaya, whose powerful initiation saved his life. Later, Baba attended English-speaking schools, where he acquired an impeccable Victorian Indian accent and perfect flowing handwriting, and then university in Calcutta.

The early twentieth century was a heady time to be a university student in a large city in British India, especially in the sciences. Baba told us he studied physics, reading or attending the lectures of many of the great physicists of the time, such as Einstein, Bohr, and Planck. The psychologist C. G. Jung came to Calcutta, too, and Baba may have heard his talks. Many of the ideas that shaped modern thought were born in those years: relativity, quantum mechanics, the unconscious mind. Baba embraced the new views enthusiastically.

Unfortunately, his father died just as Baba completed his studies. He was obliged to return to his family home and take over the family business; it was now his responsibility to provide the dowries for his eight younger sisters when they married. After fulfilling his obligation to his sisters, he was a successful businessman for many years, the owner of a chain of movie theaters in some versions of the tale, a lawyer in others. Baba told us that he never married and, despite his early initiation into Kriya Yoga, had little interest in spirituality until middle age.

In his mid-fifties, or perhaps it was in the mid-1950s, Baba had an awakening, which led him to abandon his secular life. As he tells it, while traveling down a busy Calcutta street in his limousine, Baba thought he saw Paramahansa Yogananda. Ordering his driver to stop abruptly, he leaped out of the car to follow the vision and never returned. In time, Baba's spiritual path brought him to my study in upstate New York in 1979. His autobiography, this version probably typed in the early 1970s from earlier notes, begins at the point of his renunciation.

Today is a great day for me. I received an urgent call; one may term it an S.O.S., to renounce the world, to drop out, as they nowadays say. I responded to the call in right earnestness. I renounced. In doing so, I felt as if I was not doing anything new; though I was taking a complete new course in my life, a course of which I knew next to nothing. This much, of course, I knew: that this has been the broad highway to the exclusive "Search for Self." The call resounded the resonance of my inner longing to taste divine love, in a life universal: that is what a resolve for renunciation, sanayas, indeed, meant to me. [SOS 1]*

Baba spent the next twenty or so years at the ashrams of Swami Sivananda and Anandamayi Ma, and finally at the Alakh Nath Temple of the Anand Akhara (Bliss Battalion) of Naga babas (Naked or Dragon Fathers).

His years with Sivananda were fruitful. Much of the philosophy expounded in *Crea Sadhana* echoes that found in Sivananda's books, and it was Sivananda who gave Baba his fourth and highest Kriya initiation.

Baba's three earlier Kriya initiations came from its originator, Lahiri Mahasaya, and from two Bengali Kriya yogis. The first of these is a fairly well-known direct disciple of Lahiri Mahasaya, Bhupendrath Sanyal Mahasaya.

The second is Tripura Charan Devasharma, who gave Baba the three manuscripts from which *Crea Sadhana* is drawn.

In India most families follow a spiritual tradition. Since the roots of Kriya Yoga are in Bengal, where Baba grew up, the Lahiri story could be true, though it matters little whether it is. And whatever his career, it is quite possible that he practiced Kriya, the yoga for householders, for

---

*The passage is from the first page of his unfinished "autobiography," *Search of Self.*

many years before his renunciation. Baba's physical body, his extraordinary youth and vitality, his sharp mind, the breadth of his understanding, and the power of his teaching all attest to it.

Yogananda's figure disappeared into the crowds the day Baba leaped from the limousine, but Baba's course was set nonetheless, and he never returned to secular life. In time, he found his way to Swami Sivananda's ashrams in Darjeeling and Rishikesh.

Sivananda was a good fit for Baba. He, too, had had a successful career in the secular world; he was a doctor, which appealed to the scientist in Baba. Sivananda's system of Integral Yoga was scientific, balanced, and holistic, and his ashram was orderly and calm. Baba always spoke of him with affection and great respect.

I don't know the story of how Ganesh Baba left Sivananda's ashram and went to Shri Anandamayi Ma's in Benares. Sivananda knew Ma, who had an ashram near Rishikesh in Dehradun, and is said to have called her "the finest flower that the soil of India had produced" (Bithika Mukherje, *Life and Teachings of Sri Ma Anandamayi: A Bird on the Wing*).

As the story has it, Ganesh Baba became the manager of Anandamayi Ma's ashram in Benares, perhaps from the early 1950s to the early 1960s.

*Swami Sivananda
(1887–1963)*

*Anandamayi Ma
(1896–1982)*

*Bhupendrath Sanyal
Mahasaya
(1877–1962)*

Like Baba, Anandamayi Ma was Bengali; they were roughly the same age. Born to a poor but dignified Brahmin family, Anandamayi Ma had little formal schooling and married young. Early in her marriage, she performed sadhana seriously for seven years. After that, she was recognized as a spiritual teacher, a living manifestation of the Divine Mother. Her husband became one of her most devoted disciples. Gentle, pure, and gracious, Anandamayi Ma had ashrams throughout India and many thousands of disciples. She is often listed among the major twentieth-century religious teachers in India.

Her spacious ashram in Benares sits on a ghat* overlooking the Ganges and draws many pilgrims even today. Baba's experience managing his families' chains of movie theaters was no doubt invaluable in his work overseeing the services necessary to welcome the crowds of seekers who came to see the Mother when she was still living. Spiritual pilgrimage has been big business in India for centuries and is done with remarkable efficiency. Popular temples and ashrams feed many thousands of people daily. At its height, when Baba says he was in charge, Anandamayi Ma's Benares ashram must have been a massive operation.

Yet, even though Baba was the best manager ever—he told us the accounts were perfect and the building was spotless, though countless (inexpensive, nutritious, simple, local, and completely biodegradable since they were served on leaf plates and eaten with the fingers) meals were served daily—thousands, no, tens of thousands ate there every day of the year—he was asked to leave when it became known that he was joining the Naga babas at their fires.

Naga babas—imagine them: dreadlocked, nearly naked, skin rubbed gray with ash, orange paste smeared across their foreheads—are not urban people, though they are often seen in India's cities, and some live there. Among the most ancient intact cultures in the world, Nagas traditionally live in the forests. There, they can sit comfortably around a *dhuni* (sacred fire), smoking, laughing, and exploring Lord Shiva's gift of expanded consciousness together. Baba's sophisticated background,

---

*[A broad flight of steps that is situated on an Indian river. —*Ed.*]

his university degree, his facility in English, his dapper demeanor, his many years in the urbane, intellectual city of Calcutta must all have made him very much the odd man out at the dhuni. Yet he became a true Naga, and what a wild man he was!

Though it isn't uncommon for Nagas to grow up within the community and never learn to read and write, the culture of the sadhus, Indian monks, is far from unsophisticated. Quite the opposite. The different sects of sadhus are part of a small group of exceptionally well-developed and well-preserved oral cultures, cultures many thousands of years older than our own—cultures that India, perhaps alone among the continents, has allowed to survive through her history. In fact, when I visited Baba's monastery, they were thriving.

Western culture is based on reading and writing. Oral cultures are based on memory, discourse, and the interpretation of symbols. In the West we date history from the earliest comprehensible images. We base our religions on "God's Word." *Literacy* is the key to success—and our failures are often rooted in a *literal* interpretation of the world in which we find ourselves. We believe time is linear, place great value on the past and future, and have limited faith in things that can't be proved. The Nagas, on the other hand, have little need of reading or of linear time. They memorize the long chants necessary to carry on their rituals. They live in the present, and they see form as divine instead of literal—a worldview based on ideas modern science outright rejects. Many groups, including the Anand Akhara, consider marijuana and other entheogens the gift of the greatest of gods, Shiva.

Though Baba was appointed Shri Mahant, headman, of Anand Akhara, he did not stay at the forest ashram long. Instead, he found his way back to the city.

By the time the hippies, drawn to India by the dual charms of psychedelics and Eastern philosophy, found him sharing a chillum and drinking sweet tea at Chai Baba's International Café in Benares, or sitting near the Monkey Temple in Kathmandu, Ganesh Baba was uniquely qualified to advise them.

Deborah Shri Devi

I shot this photo of Swami Ganeshanand or Ganesh Baba at his then home in Swayambhu (just outside of Kathmandu, Nepal) in the fall of 1978.

Baba in Kathmandu before coming to America
(photo by Deborah Shri Devi)

This was our first meeting; we had just come from Amsterdam with a copy of the "zine" INS and OUTS in which Ira Cohen had published the "rantings" of Ganesh Baba, and we were asked to deliver a copy to Baba. My daughter Jasmine was two years old at that time, and he had an instantaneous bond with her, telling us she was the reincarnation of his little sister Queenie who had died as a young girl.

Even though he was teaching a yoga/meditation class and his house was full of his devotees, he took us aside and shared some of his homemade bhang with us. I had never tried it and asked him for his recipe. I still have the little handwritten paper, which he wrote it on, though I never did try making it myself.

Ganesh Baba's Bhang Recipe

Cannabis leaf or flower	Nutmeg
Clove	Black Pepper
Cardamon	Saffron
Cinnamon	Sugar

Jasper Newsome

In the late autumn [of 1966] a fellow student invited me to accompany him to Darjeeling to meet a wise and charismatic holy man.

We had heard that the sage was staying at some distance from the town. Since it was already dark when we arrived, we decided to put up at a cheap boardinghouse and look for our man in the morning: but suddenly there he was, on our very doorstep. Ganesh Baba, properly known as Swami Ganeshanand, had been visiting the landlady, an elderly Anglo-Indian. We were astonished at Baba's manifesting in this fashion, but he seemed almost to have been expecting us. We took a room, and he took us in hand.

He was a short, somewhat stocky, light-complexioned man with an imposing forehead, a leonine shock of white hair, and a bushy white beard. He wore the sannyasin's orange suit of well-tailored leggings in the Nepali style, tight up to the knees, baggier above, and over them a long, loose shirt, a kurta. His cotton cap was of the lopsided Nepali variety. How old was he? About this and all autobiographical details he was to remain mysterious—this being the correct form for a sannyasin, *one who has renounced worldly ties—but he must have been seventy at the very least, though besides his white hair, the only apparent indications were toothlessness and myopia, neither of which seemed to bother him particularly. He ate only vegetarian foods save nuts, chewing vigorously with his bony gums, and without impediment spoke a fluent, often witty, sometimes haughty, always impeccable and high-flown archaic English.*

"Psychedelics without meditation is like a boat without a rudder," Baba would tell the young people. "One should not begin to smoke before the age of fifty. Such experiences are for those who have already completed their work in the world.

"But," he would admit, "since you will smoke anyway, we must make the best of it.

"First and always, you must keep your back straight! Carry your column as a column! And breathe! I tell you, buck up or fuck up!"

Anyone still slouching was kicked out of Baba's circle.

Ganesh Baba's love of physics and his taste for being at the leading edge of secular knowledge stayed with him all his life. Kriya Yoga already made the ancient science of yoga accessible; revisioning it in terms of contemporary science and depth psychology was a natural step for him.

Synthesis was Ganesh Baba's byword: synthesis of ancient and modern, East and West, science and religion, nature and spirit, consciousness and matter, Shiva and Shakti.

Several times over the course of the spring of 1982, Ehud Sperling of Inner Traditions joined us in Ovid for the weekend, eager to see the manuscripts and to move them toward publication. After the long drive up from New York City, Ehud would stand behind us watching me type and retype the first chapters of *Sadhana* as Baba made innumerable small changes, making suggestions now and then, but, considering the pace of the project, spending more time enjoying the chai and the scenery. He waited patiently then, and he is still waiting.

The long weekends often ended with all of us sitting around the fire. After the customary smoke, Baba would ask for the pages we'd finished, a single chapter rewritten so many times the pages were practically covered in correction fluid, or more likely just a page or two, in order to read them aloud. As he had during the course of the day, he found phrases that needed tweaking, ideas to add, paragraphs to rearrange. The work would not go back to New York with Ehud that weekend. In fact, Baba announced, a fresh start in the morning was needed. And with a flick of his wrist, the papers flew into the fire.

The process matters more than the product.

So, I begin this project once more, having begun it any number of times since the last time Baba and I worked on it together. I have in front of me several chapters, which I typed on an electric typewriter lent to me by my cousin, original copies marked "discarded April '82," and an older version of *Sadhana,* a carbon copy of the whole manuscript that Corinne and other students typed, every page dense with Baba's neat handwritten corrections. I remember rescuing the chapters I typed from the wastebasket the last time Baba and I worked together, tucking them into the manila folder with the older manuscript, then wrapping them carefully in an Indian scarf that smelled of Baba's snuff and tying the

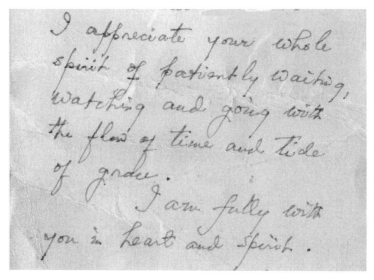

Excerpt from a letter Baba wrote to me
in September 1980

package with string, just the way he did. Ever since, I've always carried that package of papers with me or known exactly where it was; thus, that one set of papers escaped the fire that burned the rest of my copies of Baba's manuscripts. (I'm grateful to Keith Lowenstein for taking the trouble to copy a new set, page by page, on an early Xerox machine later in the 1980s.)

My own revisions of *Sadhana* have been no less prone to disappearing. In recent years, two versions were lost in two separate hard-drive crashes. Yet my original paper copy is still here, waiting, ready for me to begin again.

2
THE 4 PS

When Ganesh Baba wrote his version of *Sadhana,* the reawakening of the 1960s was at its height. A new open-mindedness had replaced the postwar emphasis on security and status quo, experiments with altered states of consciousness spawned interest in Eastern thought and practices, and the search for a new spiritual synthesis began. While Baba enthusiastically encouraged all such efforts, he saw Kriya Yoga as the missing key to the success of the movement. In retrospect, he may well have been right.

Baba's system, which he often spelled "C-r-e-a" as in creation, emphasizes balanced attention to the four phases of our being—the physical, the biological, the psychological, and the spiritual—but it always begins with keeping one's back straight. In his introduction to *Sadhana,* he writes:

Man is basically a biological being, but he is more evolved than the other species, psychically more advanced, more intelligent and conscious, rational, moral, and ultimately spiritual. It is his potential for evolution in spirituality that uniquely singles him out in the broad biological stream.

> *Anatomically, it is the vertical spine of man that structurally distinguishes him from the other vertebrates. He is the only creature in the entire course of organic evolution that has a perfectly vertical vertebra. Therefore, to reach the optimum point even of bioevolution, man is expected to carry it completely erect. It keeps the body, as well as the psyche, in optimal operational order (0^3).*

Ganesh Baba loved alliterative mnemonics like 0^3. He was a great believer in efficiency (though it was very much the Indian variety) and was fond of formulas and lists. He also believed that memorization matters and that repetition is an effective teaching method.

At the same time, Baba was a loving devotee of the Divine Mother in her manifestations as the goddesses Laksmi, personifying beauty, and Saraswati, personifying the arts.

Saraswati

Baba loved Rabindranath Tagore best of all the poets—and he loved and quoted many poets in English, Bengali, Hindi, and other languages—perhaps because Tagore (1861–1941) lived in Calcutta at the same time Baba did. The intellectual zeitgeist of the late nineteenth and early twentieth centuries in Calcutta, the Bengali Renaissance, also spawned the Brahmo Samaj movement, which uses the Upanishads to argue the ultimate monistic basis of Hinduism, and the Ramakrishna movement, which emphasizes service and the commonality of all religions. Both are synthetic movements—attempts to find common ground with the British belief system. Kriya Yoga, rooted in the same time and place, also brings East and West closer. It makes traditional Indian spiritual practice accessible to the common person, thus competing more effectively with Christianity, which was offering easy salvation to all.

Calcutta was the capital of British India until 1911. In the early-nineteenth century, it was split into parts—White Town, which was British, and Black Town, which was Indian. During the Industrial Revolution, the British invested massively in infrastructure, and a new class of urbane Indians, *Babus,* who were businesspeople, professionals, bureaucrats, Anglophiles, and world citizens, emerged. Baba must have been a Babu.

Baba's language can be romantic, lush, or lyrical, and it often over-flows with alliteration. It is a creative synthesis on many levels, like everything he did, and everything he was.

No proper perspective of perception, conception, or intelligent practice of any form of discipline, spiritual or secular, is possible without heightened sensitivity, concentration, and clarity of consciousness. Every effort for success in any field amounts to perfecting a definite discipline. Crea is a generalized discipline to perfect particular disciplines.

*Dignified Ganesh Baba visiting the New School in New York
(photo courtesy of Deniz Tekiner)*

Progressive perfection is a perennial need of Nature and Man. Most if us are, indeed, imperfect beings. We need a consistent course of exercises for obtaining optimal growth and development. The exercises of Crea are aimed at progressive perfection of each phase of our being and then the successive synchronization of the perfected phases, from the lowest to the highest, as an Integral Whole. (Sadhana, 12)

Crea Yoga, which Baba also calls "Crea-com" (an abbreviated form of Crea-communion), is a shortcut to physical and spiritual integration; the language Baba uses to describe it employs shortcuts for remembering the steps. Thus, the first four instructions in Crea are the "4 Ps," or the "4 Primes."

He speaks of posture in one of his short essays.

Proper Posture, P¹, is almost always the "anatomical position," or simply, fully erect spine. Posture and straight spine are not only somewhat symphonic* but are always synonymous in Yogic parlance. Bucked-up back is the primary pose for Proper Posture, P¹.

This is a must, continuously, without any excuse for interruption, maintained by every aspiring human being having even an iota of initial sense of the evolutionary role of man in the cosmic context. (4 Ps, 2)

Although his is not the only system to require it, Baba's emphatic insistence that his students keep their backs straight at all times singled him out among teachers and, to a certain degree, kept down the number of his students. Because it was the foundation of the practice, a quick scan of his audience revealed the dedicated students, and a hand on the back muscles indicated the seriousness of the dedication.

"Limb-limbering" is the other part of the physical practice of Crea Yoga. Ganesh Baba did not prescribe specific asanas (yoga poses), but even at an advanced age, his own posture modeled erect flexibility, and what a dancer he was! Any discipline for keeping the limbs limber would do, he told us, but it must be practiced regularly.

P¹, perfecting one's posture, is the first step in conscious evolution. Underlying Baba's theory is the firm belief in an ongoing cycle of creation and evolution, of which Darwinian evolution is only a small part.

Bioperfection is the precondition of psychoevolution, leading to the highest possible point of human evolution, in Cosmic Consciousness, or Spirit. Even Darwin drew our attention, point-

---

*Baba's language—alliteration trumps convention.

edly and graphically, in his famous ladder of evolution showing man at the top of bioevolution, to the fact that evolution
does not stop there, but is transformed into its higher evolute,
psychoevolution, to be succeeded finally by spiritual evolution.
(Sadhana, 2)

The second step in Crea is breathing: proper practice "ensures repose of respiration by rhythmic breathing."

P^2, Pranayam (regular reposeful respiration) is the most immediate and important component of cosmic pulsation, repeti-
tively reproduced as the respiration process—the most vital,
life-sustaining biological function so long as we are alive.

Its practice, therefore, amounts to plain and simple optimal reposed and rhythmic breathing. Continuous and sustained
breathing is thus a crucial condition of continuous life process
and vice versa. They are directly dependent on each other. Stop
breathing, life stops; stop life, breathing stops. (4 Ps, 2)

Another idea essential to Ganesh Baba's work, and one common to all esoteric systems including tantra, the basis of his work, is the hermetic notion of "correspondence," as in the alchemical aphorism, "As above, so below." Baba often reminded us that the Bhagavad Gita calls the human being "the mean between the microcosm and the macrocosm." The physical body reflects the cosmos.

"How can you know who the father is if you don't ask the mother?"

he asks, quoting Lalon Fakir, Baul singer and friend of Rabindranath Tagore's father. All tantra seeks spirit in nature.

Baba synopsized his teachings into a diagram he called the Cycle of Synthesis, which postulates four analogous fields in a unified field theory, combining Einstein's idea of a four-dimensional space-time continuum with Jung's notions of collective unconscious and archetypes into a framework provided by the ancient science of vibratory chemistry, tantra, and its philosophic counterpart, Sankhya, in which the fields are called the gross, the subtle, and the causal.

> That technique of "turning on" (initiation) and "tuning in" (practice), called Cosmo-com or Crea-yoga, is indeed Communion with Cosmic Consciousness through scientific synchronization of the four phases of our being:
>
> | | | |
> |---|---|---|
> | (1) physical | body | inertio-gravitational field |
> | (2) biological | life | electromagnetic field |
> | (3) psychological | mind | biopsychic field |
> | (4) spiritual | consciousness | intello-conscious field |

Each of the four Ps is related to one of the bodies and one of the fields. Posture is associated with our physical body and the inertio-gravitational field in the cosmos, and Pranayam, or breath, with our biological functions and the electromagnetic field.

The third P stands for "pinealization," in reference to the pineal gland, and is associated with the third phase, the psychological. In this step, "Crea focalizes the attention and directs it to the gyral center between the eyebrows, in intra-optical visualization" (*Sadhana*, 2)—that is, it asks the practitioner to focus his or her closed and crossed eyes on the third eye in meditation.

Baba uses another neologism for the fourth step: "pronov-mentation." The first part of the new word is drawn from the Sanskrit word commonly transliterated as *pranava,* which refers to the speech-sound, the sacred symbol OM. Using his native Bengali spelling, he creates a mnemonic for the first letters of **Pr**imordial **No**tal **V**ibration. The second part, "mentation," indicates the act of thinking. Thus, the fourth step of Crea is to repeat the word OM silently. In Baba's language, "[Crea] engages the mind in pronov-mentation, or silent, repetitive remembrance of the "Word"—"the Word that was with God, the Word that was God"—or *Sabda-Brahma* [word-God].

With practice, the student is able to perform all four steps simultaneously. Only when the four practices are synchronized, reflecting the integrated whole of the cosmos, will the key turn.

The Crea process is a direct shortcut to self-synthesis or auto-integration, what Jung calls Individuation. It is the realization of our unity with or indivisibility from the Cosmic Whole. Indeed, it is achieved by the vivid vision, at last of Cosmic Wholeness within one's self, the recognition of our true selves in the panoramic perspective of the Cosmic Self, the Radiant Reality. It happens as if by an intuitive flash of direct apprehension of the Absolute or Infinite Integral Field. In that unified or absolute field (Einstein) does our particular or individual self exist as a relative "flux." Fluxes are transformed fields; surfs indeed are transformed sea. (Sadhana, 6)

Such direct apprehension of a higher reality can happen spontaneously or through long practice, but the more powerful practices of Crea

Yoga, the real shortcuts, are passed on only orally through initiation, when the aspirant has proved himself or herself adequately disciplined and pure of heart.

This spiritual integrity, in its turn, reveals the "vision" of
U²-Intregral, Universal Ultimate Unity. Vivifying that Unitive
Vision, it embraces the All in One and the One in All, the
Everest of Evolution.

GANESH BABA'S
CYCLE OF SYNTHESIS

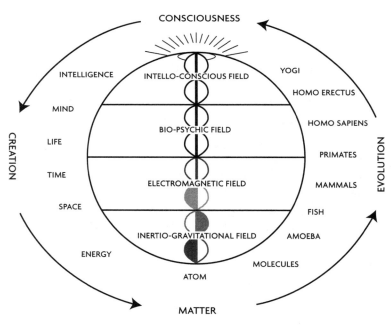

This version of the Cycle of Synthesis is the last one of many I drew with Baba. A necessarily limited, two-dimensional diagram of a multidimensional model, the significance of which I didn't grasp until my initiation, it carries within it the essence of Baba's teachings. Because it is the Akhanda Mandala, the mandala of everything, there are many, many ways to draw it.

3

COSMOS-
CONSTITUENTS

The Four Fields and the Four Bodies

I am trying to synthesize a harmonious system out of the two systems, keeping their essential qualities intact, while weaving the threads of both the analytic and the synthetic in an attempt to integrate both into a fabric of multiple texture in which the gems from all the various depths of the vast ocean of knowledge will shine out with their scintillating luster that will really herald the descension of the "supramantal" down to the common affairs of our lives.

SEARCH OF SYNTHESIS

The Crea-process is a direct shortcut to self-synthesis or auto-integration. It is the realization of our unity with or indivisibility from the Cosmic Whole.

CREA SADHANA

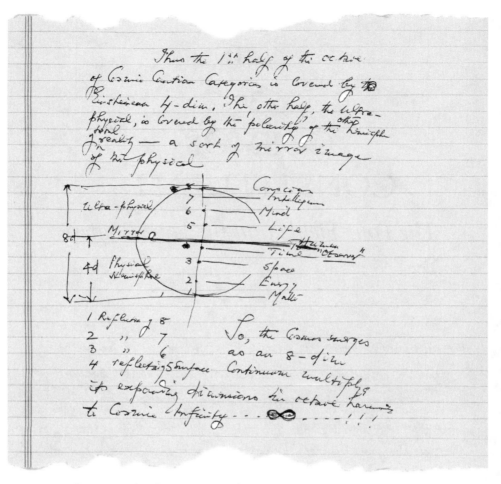

A page in one of Baba's many notebooks, probably written in the mid-1980s

What Marx called synthesis, Christ called God.

Aphorism collected by Ira Cohen, 1977

As anyone familiar with Ganesh Baba would expect, the process of writing this book continues to be fraught with the play of Ganesh.

Ganesh Baba means Father Ganesh. The name Ganesh was given to Baba when he became Swami Ganeshananda. *Ananda* means "bliss":

Little Ganesh at play

Ganesh-bliss. As a child and through his middle years, Baba used his family name, of course, but that name was long gone when I met him.

By the time I met him, in his late eighties or possibly even twenty years older than that, he was well imbued with the character of Ganesh.

Ganesh Baba crashed into our lives like an elephant, knocking down our egos and stomping all over our expectations. He delighted us with his transcendent humor. He graced us with utter generosity and wisdom more profound than any I can imagine. He ate, drank, and smoked with complete abandon. With grand passion, he recited poems and long texts. In joyful bliss, he laughed, he sang, he chanted, and he danced.

He talked through the night ("If you would be so kind, my dear, as to fill the pipe again?"), tackling every topic, explaining almost anything to anyone in language they could easily understand, though moments later his words might be equally incomprehensible. He told us stories and led us in song and dance until we were all breathless and only he wanted to go on. Then he slept for days.

Baba had a mercurial quality of reflecting back whatever he saw in us and of taking on the character of his surroundings. I recognized it only slowly. In the beginning I was terribly shocked to see him become another version of himself with other people.

When he appeared in *High Times,* I was teaching elementary school in a small town in upstate New York. The last thing I wanted was for my colleagues or the parents of the children to discover my association with the Psychedelic Swami. I didn't want to hear stories of drunken rants, yelling bouts, and intransigence in arguments. But all those stories were true. Baba could be impossible.

I was a good girl, and eager to please, and the side he showed me was kind and gentle, but he was still Ganesh. I saw him trample the egos of people who came to see him—he was not polite. Sometimes it took only a look, a look of nearly unbearable intensity. I don't think Baba read minds—perhaps he could and chose not to—but he did see auras, and he didn't mince words. As you can imagine, such intensity and plain-spokenness did not always win him friends.

Ganesh is the god of Synthesis, the child, like Jesus, of a present mother and an absent father, someone who brings together the quali-ties of two worlds. He is elephant and boy, wisest of animals and god, Wisdom and Spirit, just as Jesus is human and divine, Man and God, Father and Son, Matter and Spirit.

As the third figure in a trinity, Christ and Ganesh also represent the creative or generative principle. Abundance, represented by the god-dess Laksmi, accompanies Ganesh.

In Christianity the generative principle plays out in the story of the Loaves and Fishes, in Christ's ability to redeem all souls, and even in evangelism.

In religions with many gods, names, bodies, and stories are given to ideas labeled only as concepts in the West. These overarching concepts, called archetypes by Plato and later by Jung, are usually thought of as principles or patterns in the West, which assigns them to the abstract world of ideas. Though Western thinking creates fewer mythic charac-ters identified as such, the gods are all around us, mostly unnamed. They reside in the spirit of things, in their essence and in their commonality.

East and West agree that the Ultimate is effable and unnamable, but the two cultures treat the most subtle levels of understanding in different ways. As Ganesh Baba told us, quoting the Rig Veda, "Truth is one, but sages call it by many names." Because of their elusive conceptual nature, the gods in India are given many names and epithets to refer to their many aspects. Ganesh, a Sanskrit compound joining the words *gana* (a group, multitude, or categorical system) and *isha* (lord or master), is also called Ganapati, Pille, and Vigesha. All of Ganesh's 108 names are recited during some rituals, though often only his 12 main names are used. Thirty-two names describe his unique features. In some parts of India, he has one name for each letter of the Sanskrit alphabet.

Ganesh is associated with the first chakra, the nexus of subtle energies below the tip of the tailbone, where it is believed spiritual potential is waiting to be aroused and brought back up to the source from which it originated. He is also traditionally connected with Wisdom, represented by his elephant head, and with the mantra OM.

But, like the Greek god Mercury, and Mercury in alchemy and in astrology, Ganesh is neither here nor there, and he is here and there, all at once. His father, Shiva, the god of creation and destruction, lives in him. He is called the Remover of Obstacles, but as those of us who spent time with him well know, Ganesh's presence lights up whatever obstacles are around, so he appears to create the very obstacles he would remove. Humor and an acceptance of the unpredictable and impermanent nature of the world are part of who he is.

The gods come to Earth frequently in India. Why not? They are constantly being evoked in the spiritual practices of millions and millions of Indians. Because Indian religion is so diverse—there are thousands of gods and a massive menu of practices associated with them—and so flexible, the complex of patterns associated with given gods manifests more easily. People believe in them.

In India, in 2005, almost twenty years after Ganesh Baba's death, I saw him quite clearly in Rishikesh. After going our separate ways in the afternoon, Roxanne and I, Jayant and Sita, and Christian and Martine agreed to meet by the edge of the Ganges at dusk for *aarthi,* the nightly fire ceremony. Roxanne and I arrived first. While she looked at the wares at one of the vendors' stalls, I changed the battery in my camera. When I looked up from the camera, a small, dapper man with an elegant cane in a three-piece Western-style suit from some other era stood directly in front of me. The twinkling eyes behind his full white beard were surely Ganesh Baba's, but before I could speak he disappeared into the gathering crowd.

As I write, Baba's photograph sits near a brass statue of Ganesh on a little altar in front of me. At dawn and at dusk, whenever I can, I light a candle and a stick of incense on the altar, which is under some east-facing windows. In the morning, the candles light Baba's face until the rising sun fills the room with light. Once I opened my eyes after a deep meditation to see my own reflection blended with Baba's as the light bounced back and forth between our faces.

In the evening, the play of the candlelight often makes it look as

My face reflected in the glass on Baba's photo

if Baba's mouth is moving behind his beard. I'm not sure why Ganesh manifested in my life and the lives of my guru brothers and sisters, but I am convinced that he did, and that he still does. No doubt he is repeating his message of synthesis to me once again.

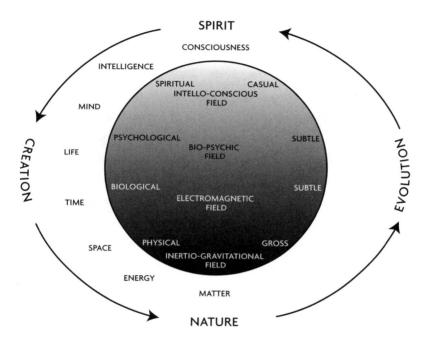

Another version of the Cycle of Synthesis

THE CYCLE OF SYNTHESIS

We often forget, in the hurly burly of our lives, our wholeness, the totality of our being. And that is the prime cause of our degradation and downfall in the world.

CREA SADHANA

Beyond the inordinate grace of showing up in my life at all, the single greatest gift Ganesh Baba gave me is the diagram, the Cycle of Synthesis.

The Sufis have a concept that describes my experience with this extraordinary diagram: *ta'wil,* in which a powerful archetypal image unfolds greater and greater truths over time. In symbolism, meaning is assigned to the image by the mind; in *ta'wil,* the image reveals its meaning to the mind.

Ovid, New York, late 1970s to early '80s: Imagine the scene. Baba, following a successful corneal transplant, comes to stay at our rambling Victorian farmhouse on a rise above Cayuga Lake, twenty miles north of Ithaca. From the wraparound porch or through elegant windows framed with delicate fretwork, you can see the sun rise over the lake.

The house was built to accommodate seasonal labor, so it has seven bedrooms, including a sizable dormitory. Baba stayed a few days and moved on, when the time was right. When he was there, the house filled up. Even when Baba wasn't there, it filled up. Children were everywhere. Hippies arrived from around the world, crazy, wise, psychedelic souls. People dedicated enough to the hippie ideals by the early 1980s and interested in a character like Baba were either hard-core idealists or hard-core heads.

Peter Meyer
From his journal from Kathmandu dated April 23, 1979

In the evening, David took me to meet Ganesh Baba—a mind-blowing evening. It was sort of a party, with half-a-dozen hippies and spiritual seekers. We began smoking hashish early in the evening and continued throughout the night. Baba hit me with everything. Today I spent the whole afternoon just getting my head together again, like the day after a heavy acid trip.

He talked a lot about fucking—said it was what we Westerners thought about most of the time. He said that my understanding of shunyata [Buddhist concept of "emptiness"] was that it was (something like) the vacuity of orgasm—only a thousand times more so. He asked me at one point, what will become of all this (indicating the phenomenal world) when I die. He said something about waking from the illusion of its reality. Said that when we were in the womb, after consciousness had arisen in the embryo, there is no awareness of space and time (these are produced by the psyche after birth). There is no awareness of light in the womb, it's like being in a dark room—but there is a night-light, and if you can remember that night-light then you know who you were before you were born.

He is incredible. He really has something. He said and did many outrageous things, and I was completely stoned, having smoked from 7:30 p.m. to 3:30 a.m. That evening I found out that there's a level of being stoned you can't exceed, no matter how much more you smoke.

In my own memory, Baba sits at my kitchen table beside a blackboard on which he's asked me to draw the Cycle of Synthesis. Someone is heating chai on the wood-burning cookstove, incense is burning in another room, and most likely marijuana. Bob Marley's voice floats in from somewhere.

The audience that evening includes a scientist or two from Cornell, several families with small children, and hippies from near and far, some far-gone indeed.

Baba at the blackboard, Ovid, New York, winter 1979

"What can you think of that you cannot fit into this scheme of things? What? Suggest anything!" Baba demands, pointing at the COS diagram.

"Love," calls out a wild-haired Australian with a stringy beard and intense eyes.

"Here!" Baba places his whole hand over the image. "It's everywhere. It's holding the whole thing together. Another one!"

"The ego?" asks someone else.

"Here," he points to the word MIND, and the evening's discussion begins. Baba is amazing. He speaks to each of us in our own language, adding words that we understand to the diagram. Baba speaks to me in Jungian primarily, but later, after he sends me back to graduate school to study creativity, he reads my sources and speaks to me in their language, always fitting any new concepts neatly into his framework.

To this day, the Cycle of Synthesis frames my worldview.

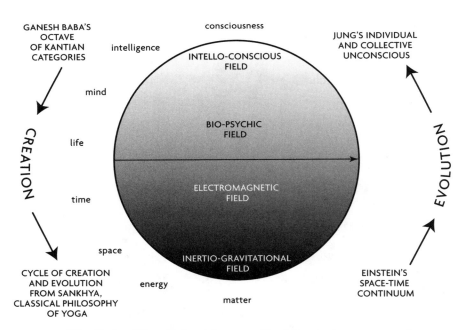

The Cycle of Synthesis with some of its historical sources noted

Baba used the term "Ganeshian Synthesis" to refer to his unified field theory and Kriya Yoga, the synthesis of ancient wisdom and modern science illustrated by the Cycle of Synthesis. He creates a continuum of Einstein's understanding of the physical world and Jung's understanding of the psychological world and fits it into a framework based on Immanuel Kant's premise that a set of categories can encompass all thought, and his own ancient Indian, orally transmitted, experience-based understanding of cosmology.

The diagram has eight dimensions. Einstein's space-time continuum takes up the lower half of the cycle, the first four dimensions. Matter and its less-dense form, energy, operate primarily in what Einstein called the inertio-gravitational field—that is, the main laws they obey are those of gravity and inertia. Space and time, the third and fourth dimensions in the theory, mostly operate in a field of subtler energy governed by the laws of magnetism and electricity, the electromagnetic field. The relationship between the fields is analogical. They are alike in some but not all ways. Magnetism and electricity have a subtler effect on the world we sense than gravity and inertia. Baba suggests that if we understand the more dense fields, we can extend our understanding to the subtler ones, including the additional two fields he proposes, the biopsychic and the intello-conscious fields.

The visible palpable universe of matter and energy is only a topographical expression of the space-time continuum in which space is the weave and time is the weft. It is a 4-dimensional continuum in which matter/energy is playing its dance of evolution in the theater of the Cosmic Space-Time Continuum.

What about the biological, the psychological, and the spiritual components of the Cosmos? As a matter of fact, what of man? What about life, mind, intelligence, and consciousness, the second half of the primordial octave of creation of the Cosmos?

FROM A HANDWRITTEN NOTEBOOK IN
CORINNE VANDEWALLE'S POSSESSION

In the years since Ganesh Baba developed his synthesis of ancient and modern science, such ideas have entered the mainstream. Baba's particular synthesis, especially at the time he first began to talk about it, may well be unique.

All forms of synthesis are sacred to Ganesh. As the third figure in a trinity, he represents the opposites that created him as well as the unique form that arises, Jung's *transcendent function*.

Central to Ganesh Baba's teaching is the synthesis of consciousness and matter, or, as he would say, the "spiritualization of the secular." The Cycle of Synthesis describes a cosmos in which matter is created out of very dense consciousness, which then evolves, through Darwinian evolution and followed by conscious evolution, back into pure consciousness. The Western scientific worldview is just the opposite; from our point of view, matter and sense perceptions are primary—most of us believe that creation begins at the bottom of the diagram.

In Baba's conception, Cosmic Consciousness, pure, formless, and subtle beyond human understanding, exists only through contrast. But through contrast, a fractal world of rainbows and musical scales is created and reiterates around us endlessly. As the frequency of the vibrating colors and tones decreases and their density increases, the world we know condenses—through the continuum of Kantian categories—into forms recognizable to our senses.

Using the words Consciousness and Spirit, and Nature and Matter, interchangeably, he explains the interaction:

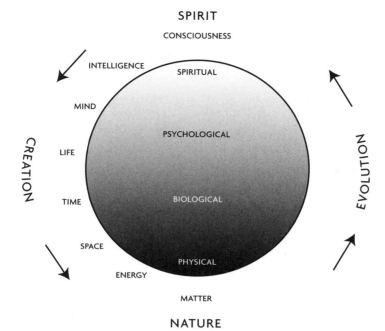

Baba's Kantian categories in the Cycle of Synthesis

Nature is negative [as in the negative pole on a battery]; power is based on the principle of potentiality and polarity. There must be a higher and lower potential, a source and a sink, to generate power, and Nature happens to be that sink. The Source is at the higher potential and the sink is at the lower end of the creative inflow—Involution. The higher potential, the Source, is positive and is termed Spirit; and the lower potential, the sink, is logically the negative counterpart of the positive source at infinity, Cosmic Consciousness. Their play of power or energy is the pulsation, or alternating, interpenetrating, vibration of the positive and the negative in their innumerable proportions and modes, permutations, and combinations.

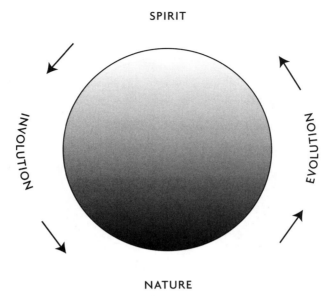

SPIRIT

INVOLUTION

EVOLUTION

NATURE

Creation and evolution in the Cycle of Synthesis

The synthesis of consciousness and matter extends to the human body. The practices of Crea Yoga are based on a holographic view of the cosmos.

In *Crea Sadhana,* Ganesh Baba writes:

In order to be harmonic, all vibratory motion has to follow this scale of "Octave" Harmonic ($2^3 = 8$): the natural musical diatonic scale. The vibratory motion or the undulatory movement is not only the common way of musical sound propagation, but it is also found to be the means of propagation of almost all other cosmic entities like light, including all electromagnetic radiation, and then biopsychic, both sensory and extrasensory: the five senses, smell, taste, touch, sight, and sound, plus thought, conception, and perception, making a full octave. Each of them, in their turn, is also geared to octave harmonics in its fundamental functions. There exists an analogous "octave" in the realm of ultraconcepts, the intello-conscious. The biopsychic is in natural tune to the cosmic rhythm of the original "octave" harmonized. So also are the intellect and the ego.

Our body reacts to that rhythm in music, to its plastic, rhythmic modulation or movement, while dancing. It is that high harmony, or lack of it, which makes for distinction, discretion, and discrimination between pairs of existential or relative polarities— dyads of dualities—such as good and bad, likable and unlikable, every scale of music, sound, sight, smell, taste, and touch.

The lilt of life, life energy, the flow of vital vibrations, also follows the natural rhythm of octave harmonics. So also the "thought-waves," or the modulations of mental energy, and intellect and ego also follow the same pattern of harmonics, the Universal Octave, the Music of the Spheres.

Cosmo-mathematically speaking, the process proceeds by the cubing of the couple ($2^3 = 8$, the Octave), the Primal Polarities or Double Dualities. "2" represents, fundamentally, the primest primordial polarity: Spirit and Nature. "3" represents the three-phased distribution of the "Primal Power" Principle: positive, negative, and neutral. The four "fields" represent the four phases of the propagation or the four broad divisions of the Unified four-fold Universe, U^3. "8" is the next term to 4 (2^2), for example, $2 \times 2 \times 2$.

In the human body, the eight categories correspond to the nerve plexii, or the chakras, which can be interpreted as levels of consciousness. Baba always smiled when he pointed out that we humans are *Homo sapiens sapiens,* man who knows he knows. To evolve beyond mind into intelligence and back to consciousness is our option as human beings, and it is more relevant today than ever.

Perhaps that's why, after so many years, the obstacles to writing this book do seem to be falling away: at least for the moment.

ᴗ3

	NATURE				SPIRIT			
	NEGATIVE		NEUTRAL		POSITIVE			
	PHYSICAL POSTURE		BIOLOGICAL PRANAYAMA		PSYCHOLOGICAL PINEALIZATION		SPIRITUAL PRONOV-MENTATION	
DO	RE	MI	FA	SO	LA	TI	DO
MATTER	ENERGY	SPACE	TIME	LIFE	MIND	MATTER	CONSCIOUSNESS
MULADHARA	SVADHISTHANA	MANIPURA	ANAHATA	VISHUDDHA	AJNA	SAHASRARA	

The Cycle of Synthesis arranged in the format of Pythagoras's Tetraktys, another traditional image of the cosmos

4

4 PS FOR THE PRESENT

From the Vedantic angle you can say this is all the Miasma of Maya, this is dream reality—you must be humble—but that does not write off our responsibility in advancing ourselves.

To individual evolution, I invite the attention of the aspirants of the world.

"The Rochester Raps," a series of interviews with Ganesh Baba, recorded by Ira Landgarten in Rochester, New York, 1980

When Americans use the word *yoga,* they're usually talking about a series of physical exercises. To Ganesh Baba and to most Indians, yoga, or more accurately *yogh,* is a much more inclusive term, often translated as the "process of yoking." In his sutras, Patanjali calls yoga "stilling the patterning of consciousness," thus associating it more closely with meditation than calisthenics. Even in the West, yoga takes many forms, some based on physical exercises, others on meditation, breath, ritual, mantra, knowledge, or service. No matter what its form, all yoga is dedicated to reconnecting matter with spirit.

The most ancient yoga practices are probably magical rituals dedicated to the goddess Kali, performed on cremation grounds where the relationship between matter and spirit is the least encumbered. In ancient times nomadic jugglers and acrobats also lived at the cremation grounds, the edge of civilization. Over time, their view of the body as temple was incorporated into the practices of Kali worship.

As yoga spread it further evolved to accommodate local cultures and their deities as well as the individual perceptions of its practitioners and teachers. As civilization became more rigid, the original strains became more marginalized, and those better suited to society found a place there.

The secrets of the old system were carefully codified so they could be passed down in their most essential form during ritual initiations. The public parts of the tradition became more elaborate. Stories emerged, and later scriptures, containing the magical secrets of reuniting matter and spirit encoded in metaphor and symbolic language.

By the time Patanjali wrote his Yoga Sutras, about two thousand years ago, a tradition of codification, essentialization, and updating passed-down teachings for a contemporary audience was well established. Ganesh Baba's work is part of that tradition, and it is within it that I begin the transmission of his teachings.

Ganesh Baba's first lesson always began with the 4 Ps. Alliterative,

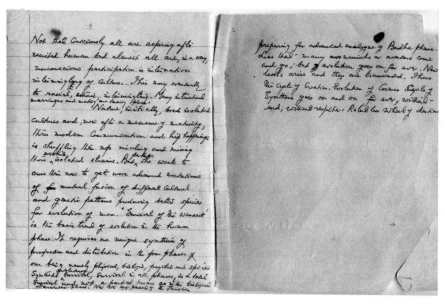

One of Baba's notebooks

numerically sound, orderly, and practical, they contain all the teachings of Crea Yoga in a number and a letter: **P**osture, **P**ranayama, **P**inealization, and **P**ronov-mentation, or more directly from Patanjali's eight-limbed (Astanga) yoga: Asana (posture), Pranayama (breath), Pratyahara/Dharana (retraction of diffused attention/concentration), and Dhyana/Samadhi (meditation/union). The closest English words for Baba's 4 Ps are probably "posture," "breath," "concentration," and "meditation," or perhaps "mantra."

Here is Baba on Astanga Yoga in *Crea Sadhana:*

Instinctive or Natural Astanga Yoga

Now, let us remember or recall our childhood, when we were very young, and ask ourselves if we had, then, any tinge of such tricky or filthy habits as violence, stealing, lying, and so on. Could we then understand theft, even if valuables were stolen away in our very presence? What deep detachment we had then. There was no sense of high or low in social level or status. We were oblivious of evil. Our mind was pure and simple: thoughts few or straight, heart-filled with the solace of self-satisfaction. We were natural yogis in union with ourselves.

The qualities of Astanga Yoga were thus ingrained in our inherent or original nature, but qualities opposed to those arose in the course of our growth and corrupted our childlike simplicity into awed adolescence and distracted, distraught adulthood and awful, frustrated old age.

For many years I worked with children's art. I think the magic in their work is *swabhava,* conformity with one's true nature, shining through. It is *Tiferet,* beauty, of the Kabbalah, the pure awareness that radiates from newborns (and enlightened beings) but is lost as babies grow up, filtered by more and more experience, buried under layer upon layer of enculturation and belief.

Swabhava is the quality that Krishna and Christ portray when they appear as babies or children: the radiant Christ child in the manger or the smiling little Krishna at play.

The Sanskrit antonym of swabhava is abhava, meaning want or poverty. Swabhava is conformity with one's true nature, and abhava represents deviation from that natural norm. Want or poverty is therefore not in the system of the universe or the normal elements of nature. It is a deviation from the natural norm.

Astanga Yoga and Crea Yoga are related to each other as the lock and the key. As a matter of fact, Crea Yoga is the universal key to all esoteric knowledge—the key to the secret code of all sciences, arts, and religions, especially the scriptures, which are written in cryptic languages with confidential codes, being handed down from guru to student. So, to yield its full potential, Astanga Yoga must be aided by Crea. Crea concerns itself with the middle four prongs of the eight-pronged Astanga Yoga.

Astanga Yoga in the Pragmatic Field

As the rustic who never knew he was all his life using English grammar, we are similarly unaware that we are using the principles of Astanga Yoga in our day-to-day activities. Apart from serving in the scientific field, the Astanga Yoga is found necessary and involuntarily brought into play in our secular efforts. As a matter of fact, Astanga Yoga is spontaneously called into action whenever there is application of concentrated mental attention. When an artist paints a masterpiece, when a mathematician delves in to a deep and difficult problem, when a scientist works on a new invention, there arises the necessity of concentrating their mental energies by withdrawing the mind from all other external objects and distractions and leading it to the particular core or field of activity in which one is immediately engaged. The method by which this is done is, by and large, the process of Astanga Yoga, but that is not explicitly understood by its users. As a result, it is observed that we are making ample use of Astanga Yoga in our secular activities without having conscious knowledge of the system.

Astanga Yoga as a technique of psycho-vital (biopsychic) concentration is used in our respective fields of action. One may improve in commercial business activities; another may become an accomplished scholar in any subject; someone else may become a great inventor. Their success has its origin in their ability to use, voluntarily or involuntarily, the principles of Astanga Yoga to withdraw their minds from distracting external influences and bring it to bear on the respective problems in an acutely exclusive, intense, and penetrating manner. One cannot even thread a small needle with acute attention without bringing this process into play.

Through Crea Yoga one may be able to bypass the step-by-step consummation of Astanga Yoga. It is like shortcutting the ascent over *a large flight of stairs by using an elevator. The use of the Crea Key automatically induces in the striver the first two angas or aspects of Astanga Yoga, yama (interpersonal) and niyama (intrapersonal). It positively internalizes the mind by focalizing the scattered vibration of a fluctuating and fumbling matter-mongering mind.*

But the striver should not be satisfied with the automatic action of Crea inducing the admirable aspects of Astanga Yoga. He must also analytically approach the aspects of systematic and careful cultivation of those aspects by concrete conscious endeavors to absorb their essence and principles of performance.

Kriya Yoga is based on the idea that if you practice the middle four of the eight limbs or prongs of Patanjali's system, the other four will fall into place. Most contemporary yoga teachings are directly rooted in Patanjali, even Buddhism, in which the eight prongs become six with different emphases and also manifest as the Eightfold Path. (Buddhism, in fact, is a prime example of an updated, adapted, essentialized yoga tradition.)

Baba's 4 Ps refer to specific practices: a straight back, diaphragmatic breathing, a concentrative form of meditation in which you look upward toward a point between your eyebrows, and the use of OM as a mantra, entry-level exercises into the world of ancient, esoteric practices.

Each of these kriyas, or actions, affects one phase of our being. P^1 aligns the body in the physical plane, P^2 in the biological, P^3 in the psychological, and P^4 in the spiritual, the four phases together creating an integrated whole.

Life evolves through each of the four phases, too. Baba believed that humanity is currently moving from the psychological phase into the spiritual phase of evolution. Unlike most of Darwinian evolution, which brought us this far, the next phase of evolution is conscious.

It is up to us whether we continue to evolve or not.

Astanga Yoga	Baba's Crea Yoga	Buddhism
Yamas	common sense	patience
Niyamas	do's and don'ts	perseverance generosity
Asana	P^1 posture	
Pranayama	P^2 pranayama	
Pratyahara	P^3 pinealization	meditation
Dharana	focusing the attention P^4 pronov-mentation	concentration
Dhayana		wisdom

Baba writes:

"survival of the weakest" is the basic trend of evolution in the human phase. It requires a unique synthesis of production and distribution in the four phases of our being, namely, physical, biological, psychological, and spiritual. synthetic evolution, survival, survival in all phases, is total survival, and not a partial process as in the biological Darwinian phase. Now we are passing the Jungian, and preparing for the advanced analogue of the Buddha phase.

In light of the tradition of updating and essentializing ancient, passed-down teachings, in grateful recognition of their source, both in time and beyond it, I offer 4 Ps for the Present:

Posture
Conscious posture and exercise

Prana
Conscious breathing and eating

Practice
Conscious Action

Presence
Constant Awareness of Consciousness

5
POSTURE
Conscious Posture and Limb-Limbering

The secret is carrying your spinal column as a column.

Lumbar should be concave.

When you are happy your posture is getting better automatically.

In India neurosis is less because posture is better. America's epidemic of neurosis can be directly traced to slouching.

"The Rochester Raps," recorded by Ira Landgarten

Because the goal of Crea Sadhana is always synthesis, the four levels of Crea Sadhana are ultimately synthesized—that is, the process of attending to one and then the next leads to practicing all four simultaneously. A balanced practice means trying to keep all four in mind while practicing each one.

Crea gives a single practice for each level, the physical, the biological, the psychological, and the spiritual, all four ideally maintained all the time (practiced always) and some dawn and dusk exercises (practiced at least once a day). The "once" exercises are carefully chosen to enhance the skills to do the "always" exercises.

Crea Sadhana begins with the physical posture—"A strong structure needs a solid foundation," Baba would say—and, of course, the constant practice is keeping one's back straight. "That alone will set you on the road to accelerated evolution," he said, but combining it with a daily morning and evening practice will focus and speed up the process even more.

> *You need not go into the animal simulations of Hatha Yoga. It*
> *will all come automatically; no need to remember the system.*
>
> "The Rochester Raps," recorded by Ira Landgarten

Ganesh Baba did not teach the physical discipline so often identified as yoga in the West, Hatha Yoga. For maintaining and stretching the physical frame, he taught limb-limbering and macro- and micromodulations.

Limb-limbering, or macromodulation, maintains the flexibility of the frame, stretching, shaking, and flexing the arms, shoulders, legs, and trunk. It is practiced every day and, in some form, before every sitting meditation. Barely over five feet tall, Baba would stand in front of us or dance among us calling out instructions.

> *Arms reaching straight up and down, alternating—high!*
> *High again!*
>
> *Shoulders pulled back and rotated—down, up, and back—main*
> *place mental complexes are stored is under the shoulder blades!*
>
> *Rotate and release, rotate and release—when the muscular*
> *system is stretched, nervous system is also being stretched.*
>
> Vieux Salydieu video

He began with the extremities. Wiggling first the fingers, then the hands and the wrists, moving into the arms and elbows, shoulders, rotating, stretching, wiggling, shaking, you can feel the life energy flowing in.

Whether you begin sitting or standing, it doesn't take long for the body to take over and tell you what it needs. With a little music, limb-limbering becomes a graceful free-form dance.

Dancing Ganesh

Micromodulation is Baba's neologism for the traditional word *mudra,* Sanskrit for "seal" or "lock," for gestures that direct energy to the brain, often using the hands. Mudras are common to all tantric Hindu and Buddhist yoga systems and are the language of Indian dance and art. In the Kriya tradition the student learns a series of mudras at successive initiations.

Baba taught one mudra to everyone, the *maha,* or "great," mudra. If we practiced it diligently, he told us, not only would our posture improve, but also our evolution would be speeded up considerably.

To perform the *mahamudra,* sit on the ground and place the left heel on the perineum. The right leg is extended at a right angle to the body. Inhale deeply and slowly, concentrating on the third eye between the eyebrows. Visualize a brilliant tube of light, the sushumna, running through the center of your body from top to bottom and exhale as you slowly bend forward to clasp your right foot firmly with both hands. (Imagine the psychic tube and not the individual chakras; with the heel on the perineum and the attention on the brow center, you will know where it begins and ends.) Hold your breath as long as you can.

Release your foot and sit up slowly, bringing the right knee to the chest while inhaling deeply. Exhale while sitting, releasing the energy into the ground. Inhale deeply, drawing energy from the Earth, and repeat the process twice more on the right and three times on the left with the right foot on the perineum, and finally three times at the center, clasping both feet.

Most days I get up at six or so and say good morning to the day and the figures and pictures on my little altar by lighting the candle and a stick of incense. This ritual is another part of the first level of Crea practice: attending to the physical space in which the practice takes place.

Here are some instructions from the original manuscript:

1) Place for spiritual practice

Find a clean room without any foul smell or other sources of distraction. Practice Crea within closed doors and not in an open place if possible.

2) Seat of Sadhana

Spread a reed mat or deeper tiger skin on level ground or on a bed. Cover it with a piece of silk, woolen material, or a blanket so that while sitting on it you will be electrically insulated from the ground. It ought to be four feet long and two and one-half feet wide, so that no part of your body should stick out while performing asana and mudras. After doing Crea, roll up the asana and do not use it for any other purpose. It is good to do daily practice at a set place unless traveling.

3) Practice of Sadhana

   First, remember the guru. Perform one round of Pranayama. Next bow, head touching the level of the seat or sitting mat. Then perform your practices serially as instructed by your yoga guru.

Although I don't have a tiger skin, even a less-than-deep one, I do use the same place every day for my practice, and before lighting the candle and incense, I roll out a small carpet. A yoga mat would serve the same purpose. I bow to the altar and thank the gurus before I begin the routine of stretches and meditation that I've done for the past thirty years.

Once in a while, I have one of those experiences when an intellectual understanding I'd had for many, many years suddenly sinks into my cells. For the past six months, there's been a new quality to my practice: I've been consciously inviting presence into it. Now, instead of going through my routine habitually with some amorphous long-term goal at the back of my mind, I try to do the exercises as if they are not a means to an end. At best, my whole attention is absorbed in the motion of my arms, or on where my waist is bending, or on the sensation of one hand touching the other. Even though doing my physical practice fully present was an integral part of what Baba taught all those years ago, it took me until recently to begin to be able to synthesize P^1, P^2, and P^3 with P^4.

Aside from practicing the mahamudra regularly, I almost always do three Sun Salutations (Surya Namaskar) each morning. During a fairly long stretch of my years teaching school, it was the only exercise I did in the mornings, no real breathwork, no meditation practice. I'm fortunate to have learned Surya Namaskar from Roxanne Gupta, who has not only practiced the series of asanas for many years but also maintained a long friendship with Apa Pant, whose father, the Maharaja of Oundh, "invented" the series. Although most Westerners think the Sun Salutation is much older, the Maharaja, with the help of his guru, combined elements of Western calisthenics with some of the mudras of Brahmanic ritual sun worship to popularize it in the early part of the twentieth century.

During our last trip to India, Roxanne collected material for a book on Surya Namaskar and sun worship, and we made a video of her performing it on the ghat in Benares at sunrise.

Roxanne Gupta

A highly learned and artistic man, the Maharaja of Oundh introduced Surya Namaskar to the world in a small book called The Seven-Point System to Health.

Ganesh Baba loved to point out that Surya Namaskar is a true synthesis of East and West. Few Westerners know, however, that there is a series of mantras that accompany the exercise, each invoking a different face, or aspect, of the sun. The Gayatri mantra, one of the most powerful sound sequences known, can also be used with Surya Namaskar.

The Gayatri mantra is most effective when recited in Sanskrit:

> *Om bhur, om bhuvaha, om swaha, om mahaha, om*
> *janaha, om tapaha, om satyam, om tat savitur varenyam*
> *bhargho devasya dhimahi dhiyo yonaha prachodayat*

You who are the source of all power
Whose rays illuminate the earth
Illuminate also my heart
So it, too, may do your work.

It took me many years to fully realize the power of the sun and the infinite potential it presents for our spiritual evolution. Consciously performed facing the earliest rays of the rising sun, with all senses present and gathered together, with full feeling, in total reverence for the source of all life as we know it, Surya Namaskar is like a door opening to another dimension, inviting light into each cell of the body.

Today, it is especially important that we change our psychic perception of the sun as an "enemy" to be protected against by screens, shades, and shields to that of a powerful source and resource: the ultimate source of life, as we know it, and the ongoing source of energy that we need to sustain life on this planet. When we start relating to the sun in terms of gratitude, the sun's full spectrum of possibility will reveal itself to us.

In addition to those two exercises, I've always taken Baba's advice and let my intuition guide the choice of exercises I do.

> **Body-wisdom will carry you through. Nature is very sophisticated. Man will never know as much.**
>
> "The Rochester Raps," recorded by Ira Landgarten

Lately my focus has been on stretches that improve posture. I return to posture again and again because of the heavy emphasis Baba put on it as the foundation of his system. Although practice of keeping one's back straight all the time isn't unknown in other yoga systems, it's more commonly only required during meditation practice. Sometimes it isn't mentioned at all. But in Crea Yoga it comes first and always. Progressive ease at holding yourself ramrod straight was expected if you want to go deeper with Ganesh Baba's system. So, over the years, I come back to it.

One morning recently I worked longer than usual on three poses that improve posture: the Mountain, the Cobra, and the Camel, a relatively new one for me that I haven't come close to mastering. I was letting my first hand drop down from my pelvis to my ankles when I suddenly understood the significance of the language Baba chose for the first of the four fields, the inertio-gravitational field.

First noted by Galileo and later restated by Newton as his first law of motion, inertia is a property common to all matter, the resistance of a body at rest to being set in motion, or of a body in motion to any change of speed or change in direction of motion.

As my hand slowly moved toward my ankle, I felt the resistance of my body, so accustomed to rest in quite another position. I tilted my thighs back a little from the perpendicular and minimally twisted to one side to get my hand onto the same-side foot. The moment my center of balance shifted, I felt gravity kick in. That's when the deep realization hit me: P^1, Posture, is about gravity and inertia.

Gravity is a more familiar notion than inertia. Gravity pulls us and everything around us toward the center of the earth, holding us firmly to the surface of the planet, causing our bodies to sag over time, creating a sense of weight. Yoga stretches are done slowly, using the breath to enhance the opening and flexing of the skeletal framework and organ systems. What I learned that morning, at a deeper level than ever before, was how yoga uses gravity to power its action.

In good posture, the force of gravity is distributed evenly through the body. No part—bone, muscle, or ligament—is stressed unduly. An engineer or architect considers the same laws of gravity and weight distribution when designing a bridge or a building. You feel lighter when your weight is balanced on and around your spinal column, and you move more gracefully.

Dan Kraak, a physical therapist and student of Ganesh Baba, describes good posture:

With good posture, you are essentially trying to lengthen your spine. With lousy posture, a slouching arch or bow, the distance from the top of your head to the base of your spine is closer or shorter than with good posture when you are sitting tall or walking tall. Turn the arch or bow into what it should be . . . the spinal column! If you are 5'8", try to be 5'9", 5'9" be 5'10". Feel a pull up from the top of your head, but toward the top/back, since most of your head is actually in front of your spine. When standing, push your feet into the ground; when sitting, push your "seat" into the seat. According to the laws of physics, for every action there is an equal and opposite reaction—as you push down, the earth pushes back, and you go up, or lengthen.

The process of perfecting one's posture over time has immense and wonderful consequences. Baba is right: posture is the foundation of sadhana. It affects and moderates every physiologic function, from breathing to hormonal production.

On the physical and biological levels, good posture opens the rib cage and gives the lungs more space, so more oxygen flows to the brain and bloodstream. Aches and pains disappear as unevenly distributed weight is balanced throughout the skeletal system. Muscles and ligaments, stressed by unnatural weight distribution, relax when poor posture is corrected. With good posture, your neck, shoulders, and upper back are not more painful or fatigued than the rest of the body at the end of a day or a long drive. Organs squashed into cramped spaces by a bent frame regain their natural shape and functional capacity.

Extra oxygen and less pain and fatigue lead to greater concentration and mental ability. Thus the physical field affects the biological and the psychological fields. Baba often explained that the central nervous system runs through the spinal column and is like an antenna. Depending on the direction it points, it picks up different signals. Poor posture connects to lower frequencies than good posture. With head held high and shoulders back and down, one not only sees a different world from the one a slouched person sees but also tunes in to, as Baba put it, a different radio station. As Dan Kraak observes, "Baba taught that poor posture produces static that interferes with the reception of finer transmissions. By having good posture, you are producing an optimal antenna for tuning in for proper reception."

Imagine the shift in consciousness that is inherent in these two postures. You literally see two different worlds, and others see you either as confident, competent, vigorous, and youthful, or as burdened by the weight of the world. Baba liked to point out that the secret of good posture is well known to both the military and the aristocracy.

Neither paying attention to my posture nor the inclination to do physical exercise comes naturally to me; I've spent a lifetime overcoming inertia and gravity. Over time I discovered that the key to preventing habitual sloppy posture is not to get locked into it. Dan suggests a visualization exercise: "at least five minutes of daily visualization (checking yourself in a mirror occasionally) of yourself with good posture in addition to trying to maintain it all day will reprogram your biocomputer. You generate a Proper Posture Program (another P^3) using mental imagery, as employed by musicians, athletes, and dancers. As the new program runs, when you fall, it will snap you back sooner and sooner."

Now, twice a day whenever I can, I take the time to work at strengthening the muscles that keep me straight and flexible. Throughout the day I remember my intention to stand and sit straight, and I stretch and correct my stance often. Good posture shouldn't look or feel stiff or awkward. A short, concentrated period of working at keeping the back straight and flexible will add dignity and grace to anyone's appearance, and the evolutionary cycle will kick in.

If, in the end, you learned nothing from Ganesh Baba except to keep your back straight, he would be satisfied.

Bas.*

---

*"Sufficient" in Hindi.

6

PRANA

Conscious Breathing and Eating

> *The capacity for resonant "rapport of reception" is always there, but due to interference of the unwanted, superfluous vibrations of the mind, and consequent development of "static" in the life-pulse resulting in an unrhythmic respiration pattern, the rapport is enfeebled or almost lost. Reestablishing that rapport by scientific simulation of the natural rhythmic, reposed respiration by Crea-pranayama is the main mode of Crea Yoga. Other adjustments or actions are, of course, also there.*
>
> Ganesh Baba

Ultimately, my experience with Ganesh Baba and his teachings is a story, and like all stories, it changes a little every time it is told. Stories can't help but take on the personality of their tellers and the perspective of the culture and time in which they are told. Experienced storytellers say the trick to telling a story well is grasping its structure and letting the details tell themselves.

Several chapters of this book were written and the transcription of the manuscript completed when Ganesh set up some obstacles for me. At that time my plan was that most of the book would be Baba's writing. Who could say it better? I would add a little commentary, a few anecdotes, and a summary chapter or two at the end. During the months when I was transcribing, I practiced Crea at dawn and dusk, sometimes putting in as many as three hours a day, almost always giving it a couple of forty-minute periods.

The winter the transcription was done, I traveled to India with Roxanne.

Jayant Gupta Meets Ganesh Baba

I met Baba in 1966 and didn't like him at first. This "dislike" continued through the winter of 1970. He didn't fit into the traditional monastic order of things—he spoke very good English, ate at restaurants, hung around with many pretty Western women—in a word, doing all the things sadhus are not supposed to be doing. I thought he was pulling a fast one to impress the Westerners by calling himself a Shri Mahant. Many of my Western friends wanted me to at least sit down with him for an hour or so, listen to his rap, smoke a few chillums with him . . . well, ever since then, he has been with me in my world, even after his death . . .

We traveled by train to Bareilly where we visited Baba's Samadhi at Alakh Nath Temple. In India most people are cremated. Only those who die a "yogic" death are buried. Though he died at Nanital in the fall of 1987, Ganesh Baba wanted his body transported to the Anand Akhara monastery at Alakh Nath, where he was once headman, or Shri Mahant. His body is buried sitting upright in a small temple, or Samadhi, with a handsome statue of Ganesh in it.

Visiting the Akhara was a treat. In India a few years earlier, I'd attended a dinner party in New Delhi where the conversation came around to the economic boom in India. The woman seated next to me

Ganesh Baba's Samadhi at Anand Akhara
(photo by Eve Neuhaus)

took it philosophically. "India survived the Moguls, India survived the British, and India will survive Western culture," she said.

By the time of this visit, the boom was so pervasive that it was easy to wonder if India would survive. Shopping blocks were full of Western-style shops: TGIF, The Gap, KFC. Western clothing was as common as Indian in many parts of the big cities. Cell phones had become a real nuisance. But who would have thought the boom would have reached Bareilly? It turns out that Bareilly's location between Lucknow and New Delhi made it a very hot place for development.

The boom even hit Alakh Nath. Three years earlier the rickshaw ride to the rural temple took us over dark, rural lanes to a temple that seemed old and somber to me. The toilets were the worst I saw in all of India, where toilets can be pretty awful. The babas, dreadlocked, near-naked, and coated in ash, their faces painted with yellow, white, and orange stripes, welcomed us kindly and asked us to join their circle, but none of them spoke more than a few words of English. No one remembered Ganesh Baba personally. It was hard to visualize him as the head-man of such a place.

Imagine our surprise on this visit when, on reaching the temple just after dark, we were greeted by a brightly lit statue of Hanuman at least thirty feet tall. More changes greeted us inside the temple gates. Even in the dark, you could tell things were cleaned up. And there at the main dhuni sat Balak Baba, a friend to all Ganesh Baba's friends. His loving energy affected the whole akhara. It was full of joy!

Not to mention new buildings. We sat at Saloney Baba's dhuni, too, and there we met the young man responsible for all the changes, a local fellow in the business of building shopping malls but completely dedicated to the babas. After that evening of laughter, smoke, stories, and song, I could see why Baba chose to return there for his Samadhi.

Following our visit to Alakh Nath, we stayed on the ghats in Benares where Baba lived so many years at the ashram of Anandamayi Ma and later as a Naga baba hanging out with Western hippies.

Finally we soaked in the intellectual Victorian essence of Kolkata, where Baba lived most of his adult life before his renunciation.

Yet on my return to California, I found that instead of increasing the creative flow necessary to writing, my trip to India seemed to have stopped it. It would be many months before I found the new understanding that let me continue working on the book.

The language and understanding of the first level of practice, Posture, is very close to what Baba taught. It is at the second level that the structure begins to take on new details. Ganesh Baba calls the second P of the 4 Ps of Crea Yoga "Pranayama," but it is called Prana here. *Prana* is vital energy, the energy of life, and *yama* means "control."

Pranayama is the fourth limb of Patanjali's Astanga Yoga, control of the breath. Using the word *Prana* instead of *Pranayama* broadens the understanding of the second level of practice to include conscious eating and attention to the life energy all around. With P¹, we bring consciousness through the mechanism of attention to the physical frame and our physical surroundings. With P², we bring consciousness through the mechanism of attention to the biological field, to our flesh and blood, to the life within and around us.

In *Crea Sadhana,* Baba writes:

> *"Life energy"—biopsychic energy analogous to electromagnetic energy—prana—is a subtle organizing principle, a creative force, a synthesizing power. Its most important function is to maintain the combination of the gross functions on one hand and the subtle-causal on the other. It is a link between the gross matter-energy and the causal Spirit-Consciousness.*

The terms *gross, subtle,* and *causal* come from the Indian tradition. Usually translated as the three "bodies," they can be understood as three densities of energy (and thus consciousness), or as three worlds. Using the word *causal* for the most subtle form of energy illustrates the understanding that creation begins beyond the subtle and ends with the gross, the form of energy that can be detected by the senses.

The three worlds show up all over the globe under many names, with different varieties of images hanging from the branches of their world trees: the cross, the Bo tree, the spine, the tree of knowledge, and

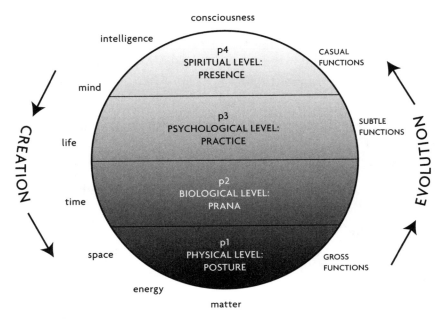

Another version of the Cycle of Synthesis

the tree of life. In some times and places the three worlds are the underworld, the middle world, and the upper world; in others they are hell, Earth, and heaven.

There are countless iterations of these primal patterns: the huge polarities, good and evil, feminine and masculine, and the like; and the huge triplicities: positive, negative, neutral; body, psyche, spirit; solid, fluid, gas; Father, Son, Holy Ghost; and in alchemy: salt (fixed), mercury (mercurial), and sulfur (active). The polarities and the triplicities are all continuums, whether they have mythic names or scientific ones. They represent the spectrum of consciousness divided into two in the case of polarities, and three in triplicities, overlapping regions. They are the patterns through which we see what we perceive to be "the world."

Perception gives form to the physical world, not the other way around.

From *Sadhana:*

The subtle-electromagnetic and biopsychic bodies supply the required power to the gross, biological or biophysical body so it can perform its biophysical and biopsychic functions.

Prana, carried by the breath and the food we eat, is the connection between the mind, intelligence and consciousness, and the physical body. The body cannot do work without energy supplied by the breath and food.

Because it connects body and mind, the emotions are closely connected to breath. Without thinking, across cultures, we breathe shallowly when we're stressed, gasp when we're frightened, exhale when we're exasperated, and release a sigh of relief when things are okay again.

At the P² level, Crea Yoga once more recommends a single simple practice to be done constantly, or at least as often as you can remember to do it: deep, slow breathing. Baba called it "relaxed, reposed respiration." Every breath, he said, should fill the abdomen.

> When you're sad, breathe deeply.
> When you're stressed, breathe deeply.
> When you're angry, breathe deeply.
> When you're anxious, breathe deeply.
> When you're happy, breathe deeply.
> Breathe deeply.
>
> ROXANNE GUPTA,
TEACHING CREA YOGA

Becoming conscious of your own breathing patterns and making the effort to lengthen and deepen your breath even once in a while is a simple and remarkably effective strategy for improving your life. Even one person breathing slowly and deeply in a stressful situation where others are taking shallow, unconscious breaths will change the atmosphere.

When good posture and full attention to the situation at hand are added to the mix, even bigger shifts take place. Finally, an attitude of nonresistance and open-mindedness allows pure consciousness to flow into the most seemingly intransigent circumstances. Straightening up your shoulders and taking a few deep, slow breaths begins the process of change.

Relaxed, reposed respiration is practiced at greater depth and with greater control during the dawn and dusk practice period but follows the same pattern. Draw in the air through the nostrils until it fills the lungs completely, expanding the abdomen and diaphragm to let in the greatest amount of air. I imagine that my body is like a balloon that I fill with my breath. Exhaling is just the opposite. Breathe out long and slow, drawing in the abdomen, raising the diaphragm, and emptying the lungs as completely as possible. Squeeze out the air methodically as if emptying the balloon slowly and thoroughly. The outgoing breath should take twice as long as the incoming breath.

For general balancing, breathe evenly. Prana is ingoing breath. Apana is the outgoing. They should be equal so they neutralize. The ingoing breath takes in less because of atmospheric pressure. Outgoing must be slowed down. If you maintain a 1:2 ratio, out to the count of 8, in to the count of 4, you even out the breath.

"The Rochester Raps," recorded by Ira Landgarten

Another kind of breath is also prescribed only for the practice period. Baba calls it jet or spurt breath and describes it as "decarbonization with lumbar flexion." A cleansing breath, jet breath is a series of rapid exhalations with no emphasis on inhalation. With each breath the lumbar region is flexed and the diaphragm is lifted to push out the air. "Inhalation takes care of itself," Baba explained. These quick breaths are repeated until you feel a little dizzy from hyperventilation. The hyperventilation alters consciousness just enough to ease the transition into a trance state with the longer practice of long, slow, deep breaths.

Baba's instruction for the deep breathing is simple: "Take as many of the longest, slowest, deepest breaths you can," he told us. Every time you lose track of the deep breaths, revert to jet breaths—a few will do—and then return to long, slow, deep breathing.

After taking several of the longest, slowest, deepest breaths you can, begin to hold your breath for a few moments at the end of each inhale and again at the end of the exhale. Slowly increase the number of times, the length of the breaths, and the length of time you hold your breath until you can do about twelve very long, slow deep breaths without retention and another twelve with retention. Increase the amount of time you hold your breath over time.

After the very deep breathing, continue with rhythmical, reposed respiration, until the end of the practice.

Breathing consciously is a marvelous experience. Stretching the lungs is as pleasurable as stretching your arms and back when you wake up in the morning. A good dose of oxygen clears the mind and relaxes the body.

The benefits of taking extra oxygen are well documented. Patients in hospitals are given oxygen after surgery because studies prove it fights infections. It's been known for many years that oxygen relieves stress and increases mental power. In a recent study in Britain, volunteers remembered up to 20 percent more words from a list after they were given a short blast of oxygen through a facemask.

As a result of such studies, purveyors of oxygen machines are doing very well right now. A little extra oxygen, available in cans or in machines you can set up in your home, provides almost immediate relief for headaches, hangovers, migraine, stress, fatigue, cramps, jet lag, heat exhaustion, or minor aches and pains. Oxygen bars, where customers order a cylinder of the gas with their drink, are fashionable the world over. Oxygenated water is too, though studies show that a bottle provides less useable oxygen than one deep breath, which, of course, is free.

As birth educators and other pain experts will tell you, gaining control of the breath can give you power over pain as well as over emotions. Two of my children were born before I learned to breath consciously from Baba and two after. The difference I experienced was remarkable. Not only was the pain of the births reduced to an intense feeling of tightness, but I also felt much more in control of the whole experience.

Remembering to breathe more deeply during the day is easier if you identify a place or a situation where you always try to take a few deeper breaths—for example, as you pass through a certain door, go up a flight of stairs, when you are in the elevator, or in the shower. Using a location to stimulate memory is a well-proven strategy.

Even one conscious deep breath makes a difference. Two or three are even better. Practicing pranayama in the morning and evening doesn't cost a cent and gives palpable results in a short time—after just a handful of practice sessions you will find your normal breathing patterns beginning to change.

Ganesh Baba came of age in the time of empiricism, a period still going on, when it is very important to be scientific—hence the name of his loosely formed organization, the Scientific Spiritualization Society—so Crea Sadhana builds upon itself in a logical, scientific way. As keeping your back straight opens the rib cage to allow more air to fill the lungs, thus sending more oxygen to the brain, so conscious breathing sends even more oxygen to the brain, which relieves stress and builds mental acuity. P^1, the physical, affects P^2, the biological, and P^2 affects P^3, the psychological.

From the manuscript:

Pranayama is the scientific yogic technique of the harmonization of the "mind" and "life" pulses. It organizes the relative rhythm of life and mind and brings them in perfect unison with the streamlined motion of psychosomatic energy (Chitta

Vritti Nirodha). Patanjali defines Pranayama as progressively increasing the gap between "inspiration" (inhalation) and "expiration" (exhalation).

We also take in prana, life energy, through eating. Though Ganesh Baba claimed to be a member of every religion and told stories of his time as a devotee of Islam and Christianity ("I was known as Father George as a Catholic and Father Gnossos in the Orthodox Church"), he grew up Hindu in Bengal and ate like a Bengali; he didn't eat meat, but dairy products, eggs, and even some fish now and then were all okay. Peter Meyer recalls Baba's general rule: "If an animal can cry for life, don't eat it." (Fish and eggs don't cry out.) I can hear him extolling vegetarianism to his American students, describing the cries of animals about to be slaughtered or explaining the value of a diet of micromolecules rather than macromolecules, which clog up the subtle channels.

Here is the advice on diet *Crea Sadhana* gives:

Reversal from the gross material to the spiritual involves an initial return to purity in food and character. This purity in food and other habits is necessary for evolution into the higher life of mental, moral, intellectual, and spiritual perfection. A succulent, pure, ennobling vegetarian diet is ideal for the aspirant or sadhak. One can certainly develop a taste for those pure stuffs by a little strength of mind, a little compassion for life and some sense of equity and abstinence from associating with the cruelty of animal killing. An intense feeling of decency should be sufficient to counteract the corrupt practice of relishing the coarsening carcasses of killed animals. Putrid food perverts human nature—perversion brings profanity. Profanity leads to cynicism and frustration. Frustration gives rise to moral imbalance and spiritual nullity.

Moral laxity and spiritual crisis are the twin products of wrong and improper habits that have now invaded all aspects of human behavior.

It is clear we cannot attain spiritual purity with coarsening and enervating or exciting food intake. There is no other mode or method of basically attaining the balanced state of equilibrium and equanimity without refraining from taking corrupt food. If not for any other reason, one single evil, the bad food habits of the modern man, is good and strong enough to deviate him from the course of refined equilibrium, morality, and spiritual elevation. We are sparks of divinity, sons of God, the apex point of known evolution. But now we have put the crawling worm to shame in our animality or beastliness of our food habits. We have lost the paradise. We have fallen from our rightful state of our native nature (swabhava), of subtle and refined living in amity with all life, with which we have a direct biological connection.

Later, in a summary near the end of the manuscript, in a section that sounds like it's probably a close translation from Sri Tripura's original Bengali text, Baba says:

Diet

Balanced diet, simple, light, luscious, clean, and nutritious food must be taken. It must be easily digestible within about three or four hours. Over- and undereating must be avoided. It is better to eat less at night than in the daytime. It is necessary to take enough milk and milk products such as yogurt or curd, butter, and cheese. Regularity in the time of meals must be maintained.

Once again, Crea takes a balanced approach.

Today, vegetarianism (and more so veganism, which eliminates all animal products, including dairy and eggs) is a chic, social, and political action as often about saving the earth and its inhabitants as it is about spiritual evolution. With changing economic realities, the value of fresh, local foods is being rediscovered, and an exciting revival of the raw-food movement is taking place.

Roxanne Gupta on Raw Foods

The raw-food movement is the spiritual revolution that Ganesh Baba never lived to see. Nonetheless, Baba's own dietary habits foreshadowed the rising consciousness of the connection between what we eat and who we are. (This despite the fact that he sometimes broke many rules when it came to his own consumption!)

In 1978 I bought one of the first copies of Viktoras Kulvinskas's now classic tome, Survival in the 21st Century (the first manual of a holistic raw-foods lifestyle), which Baba avidly read. He declared that this book was "fantastic." I myself was fascinated with the idea of raw foods and underwent various juice and water fasts but ultimately was too bound by Indian culture (having recently become vegetarian after living in South India for a year and marrying into an Indian family) to consider such a radical step.

It had taken me a few years to expand my repertoire of Indian dishes and to understand the "hot" and "cold" theories about which foods were to be eaten in which seasons. Through this avenue I had entered into the world of [Frances Moore Lappé's] Diet for a Small Planet and began making the connection between environmentalism and food. At The New Delhi, the vegetarian restaurant we opened in Geneva, New York, that became Ganesh Baba's first base of operations in America, I prepared all kinds of ethnic foods using whole grains and healthful ingredients, departing drastically from the traditional Indian mainstream.

Indian cuisine is vast, with many regional, caste, and class variations. Caste is bound up with the idea of "pollution," and traditionally caste rules determined not only what one eats but also with whom one eats. The poor may live on two rotis (flat breads) a day, while the rich will drink cream. In terms of health, the traditional Ayurvedic system centers on the three doshas [constitutional types], which makes one's diet highly individualistic; but only those who have enough to eat can afford to be discriminating. For this reason, Kriya Yoga could not explicitly advocate any particular dietetic formula beyond the idea of vegetarian sattvik (calming and balancing) foods: if one is undertaking spiritual discipline, one needs to maintain "purity" in body and mind.

Dairy products were the staple of the Indian diet for thousands of years; as the old theory goes, during the Aryan migration, mobile herds were what enabled the tribes to travel across continents. The cow has been sacred because life on the road and in settlements depended on her five products: milk, yogurt, ghee for cooking and for lamps, cow dung for fuel, and urine used in building and in some medicines. Indian civilization was built upon the foundation of the cow. To this day, *those who eat the most traditionally sattvik or strict diet will eschew onions and garlic but load up on dairy products.*

Kriya Yoga was an upper-middle-class phenomenon that reflected the Bengali sensibility of its founder, Lahiri Mahasaya. Designed for "householders," it was circumscribed by the newly emerging values of the Bengali Renaissance, the cultural movement that resulted from contact with the British. Like so many other religious movements of its time, it sought to adapt traditional Indian values and spiritual techniques to a modern era of rapid social change. Dairy products were considered a central and important part of the diet, both for traditional reasons and because dairy was considered sattvik, or pure. Although they add pounds, the Indian aesthetic considers a voluptuous body a sign of health and success, while a thin body has the association of poverty and asceticism. Kriya Yoga, being an adaptation of yogic techniques for householders, advocated a "middle path" to body weight, as well as diet.

Although he stood in the Kriya line and was himself Bengali, Ganesh Baba relied more on science than on tradition, even though he was thoroughly versed in both. To his disciples he advocated vegetarianism, but he himself would occasionally eat fish. He advocated wholesome organic foods but was not above eating diet ice cream and [drinking] Diet Pepsi! (Baba's Ganeshian sweet tooth had resulted in an early onset of diabetes.) Nonetheless, he insisted on taking fresh green salads every day, which, due to his teeth, I would have to put in the blender so that he could drink them: he was drinking green smoothies without knowing it. Once when he was hospitalized his doctor admonished me, saying, "I don't know how much insulin to give him because I don't know what food you are bringing him. Everything you bring him is green!" Baba also took a slew of vitamin supplements every day, sometimes as many as thirty.

If he were alive today, I believe that Ganesh Baba would be a huge advocate of the raw-foods movement as by far the most appropriate diet for those doing Kriya practice. Following the teachings of

Gabriel Cousens and Viktoras Kulvinskas, we can envision the raw-foods movement as the next evolutionary step for those who want to retain their humanity, for those who want to remain firmly grounded in the terra firma rather than "blast off into space." A raw, enzymatically rich, alkalizing diet based on living, green "superfoods" results in a process of human photosynthesis capable of transforming us at the cellular level. The ramifications of such a diet are literally mind blowing. Not only will such a diet feed and transform our bodies and consciousnesses, it will transform our society and our relationship to the planet.

How many pounds of grain does it take to create one pound of animal flesh to be consumed after an act of violence? That same grain could feed ten times as many people. Now take the same grain and sprout it, and it exponentially increases the number of people that could be fed from the same amount of grain. Of equal importance to quantity is quality. Literally and metaphorically living on light, humans are capable of transforming themselves into embodied light-beings. The raw-foods movement is a process of Ganeshian synthesis writ large on the planet.

Bridging the biological and psychological levels of sadhana is singing. One of the three manuscripts Tripura handed down to Baba was entirely on *Bhajan*, the singing of devotional songs.

sadhana, as we have seen, makes for spiritual experience.
Bhajan, on the other hand, makes for spiritual expression.
Inner experience and outer expression must go hand in hand
in any integrated process of self-evolution or fulfillment.
Therefore Bhajan or singing the holy hymns must accompany

sadhana. Experience without expression can be stultifying.
Expression without experience is empty.

Singing is a musical mode. It has its harmony and melody.
Harmony imparts rhythm and development of a sense of rhythm
and reinforces the Pranayama process. Melody mellows one's nature
and counterbalances hardening and harshness. It elevates the
emotional level and lifts its "feeling" to higher harmonies of the
Cosmic Symphony, in which we are all insignificant coplayers in the
Cosmic Concert.

Into the text of the Bhajans are woven the experiences of prior
Sadhaks. Therefore singing them enhances and confirms the ethos of
one's own experience. It makes for better balance and equanimity.
Therefore Sadhana and Bhajan must go together. Their combination
is satisfying and fulfilling. Otherwise the Sadhak will be lopsided.

Every language has spiritual songs and music. So, there is
no dearth of singing material for the Sadhak, whatever may be
his mother tongue. Hymns, sonnets, elegies, or any song will do
for the practice of Bhajan. Collective singing is also good for this
purpose.

In the presence of our group of friends, Baba often divided the
population between "psychedelics" and "beefy-alcoholics." The psychedelics were due to inherit the earth, while the beefy-alcoholics
ate and drank themselves to death. Two of his best-known aphorisms
are "Beware of the nonpsychedelic" and "A nonpsychedelic can never
enlighten a psychedelic." Beefy-alcoholics were clearly to blame for
most of the world's problems. Baba told us that eating beef increases

aggressive behavior, and drinking alcohol changes the frequency of one's consciousness in the wrong direction. It was a pretty black-and-white picture. Being of the psychedelic bent myself, I felt comforted by these statements until I heard a story of his drunken rampages in New York City. I didn't understand then that Baba reflected the color of his surroundings.

It's difficult to understand why such behavior doesn't amount to hypocrisy to me, but after many years of wrestling with my thoughts and feelings about this aspect of my relationship with Baba, I've come to the conclusion that it doesn't matter. By calling it hypocrisy, or even disingenuousness, I attach a derogatory label to a behavior that is beyond my comprehension, part of a higher level of organization that appears "wrong" or "chaotic" only from my limited viewpoint. Probably Baba got drunk with some people to teach them something. Who am I to judge?

Can a legitimate charge of moral relativism be brought to such an argument? It's hard to say. Ganesh Baba was like the god he represents, mercurial, impossible to pin down. I believe he was a "crazy wisdom" teacher in the Buddhist understanding.

Robert Sachs, author of *The Passionate Buddha*, on crazy wisdom teachers

When talking about "crazy wisdom," we first need to divest the term crazy from connoting insane or mindlessly bohemian. And we need to understand the word wisdom, which is, in fact, the domain of the feminine. In the Buddhist word male energy perfects itself in the expression of skillful means—accurate and well-executed action. Female energy perfects itself in the expression of a discernment that always has as its goal nurturance of what promotes growth—bringing out our best. When skillful means and wisdom come together, you have the compassionate acts of an enlightened being.

So what then does it mean when we attach the word crazy to the word wisdom? What we are speaking about is a perspective that is not unconventionally focused on bringing out our best but rather beyond convention in bringing out our best. Thus, for our benefit, all cards are on the table. A "crazy wisdom" teacher could wear a three-piece suit, a loincloth, or be completely naked for that matter. Their sole purpose in whatever guise they present us with—their words and the actions they display—are to create the optimal circumstance for our awakening. For in the end, it is the box we put ourselves and our world in that is the greatest impediment to our growth. The crazy wisdom teacher offers no resistance to the box and thus allows it to explode of its own accord. What is also the case, in a more relative way, is that each teacher has his or her own style, which attracts the kind of disciple that best learns from and will be transformed by his or her action. A teacher who attracts psychedelic students will stretch them beyond their limits in their psychedelicness. A teacher who attracts beefy-alcoholics will do the same. In either case, the crazy wisdom teacher can never be pinned down because no reference from the past guarantees what happens in the moment. That said, however, such a teacher also has the skill to know how to ground the experience so that his or her students maintain a mindfulness to the process of their awakening, no matter how pleasant or painful that process is. If the teachers cannot do this, then they are truly not crazy wisdom teachers and are, at worst, charlatans of the heinous sort.

In Tantra, if one is a meat eater, we give him so much meat he will ask for dal and chapati.

Ganesh Baba at the Kumbha Mela at Allahabad, 1977,
collected by Ira Cohen

Ganesh Baba never had a big following. His attempts at organizing his followers amounted to little more than the handwritten heading "Scientific Spiritualization Society" written on some notes and letters. In fact, he had very little good to say about the large organizations that grew around other teachers. He traveled from place to place with one or another of us, carrying his few belongings with him. There was no plan; he went wherever he was invited, rarely staying in one house for more than a few days or weeks. Baba did maintain correspondence with old friends and once in a while called on one of us to come for him and take him to his next destination.

Corinne Vandewalle

It was Ganesh Baba's unusual friendliness, his approachability, his sense of modesty, and above all his all-embracing love—his rejection of the traditional and lofty distant pedestal—that won him such popularity among the love-not-war New Age Generation Advance

Ganesh Baba and Corinne Vandewalle
(photo courtesy of
Corinne Vandewalle)

(NAGA), the flower children. Yet all attempts to install him in ashrams, societies, missions, and groups of all kinds failed. His Naga nature was always more strongly drawn to the high winds of liberty, equity, and liberation from human bondage!

Judy Brown

I spent only a short time in Baba's company, when I visited Eve while he was staying there. He was very kind to me and gave me a sort of crash course in the important things: straight spine, oxygenation and decarbonization, limb-limbering, and the like. He certainly knew things about me and my life that went beyond the superficial, and he gave me some very pointed and timely advice. Baba had such a reputation for being hard on his students that when I told people he had been kind to me, they looked concerned—that's not good, they said, as if his level of anger and criticism indicated his degree of caring. As a powerful teacher, I think he took the task most effective to open the door for each student—that's how it felt to me.

7
PRACTICE
Conscious Action

The working title of this book was always *Crea Sadhana: Crea,* Baba's spelling of *kriya,* the Sanskrit for "action," combined with the English word *creative,* and *sadhana,* which means "means of realization" or "spiritual practice," thus "creative spiritual practice." Yet even months of intensive practice combined with close to thirty years of erratic practice seemed like it wasn't going to be enough to write a book with a title like that, a book handed down from my guru's guru to him and then to me. Who was I to write a book on creative spiritual practice?

The months after I returned from India, I practiced morning and night, I tried to keep my back straight and to breathe deeply all the time, but the words didn't flow out of my fingers. Creativity isn't something that comes from trying. It comes by grace. I set up a tidy schedule: Crea at dawn, breakfast and dog walk, few hours of writing, an hour of housework or gardening, more practice, then cooking, and so on, but my connection to my muse was gone. I could go through Baba's material, I could listen to recordings of him speaking on my iPod as I worked around the house, but I couldn't translate it onto the page. Finally I sat in front of my altar in frustration and gave up completely. Maybe I wasn't the person meant to write the book after all.

The reality is that this kind of material has to ripen; sometimes there is no option except patience. The transcript needed to be brought up to date in ways I hadn't anticipated, and I didn't know how to do it. I waited and practiced some more.

The inspiration for a new approach, the new four Ps, came to me in a reasonably timely way. I was thrilled when the new language for the four Ps arrived during a meditation. At that time, I was using the quaternary "posture, breath, concentration, meditation" or "posture, prana, concentration, meditation" for the four levels of Crea Sadhana. I knew that Baba's fourth P, *Pronov-mentation*—ceaseless, soundless repetition of the mantra OM—the practice associated with the god Ganesh was a portal to a state of consciousness that comes only by grace.

It was not a big leap to recognize that the fourth P could also be called Presence. But when the word Practice came to me as the third P, my understanding came more slowly. And I still found myself unable to get much of anything down on paper.

Because of the manuscript title, *Sadhana,* I'd been playing with the idea of practice, spiritual and otherwise, for years. When I taught school, I was a big proponent of practice—my students had to do more exercises in math and writing than most—because I felt so strongly that practice improves performance. Once I committed to bringing the manuscript and Baba's teachings to publication, I knew it was time to get more serious about my own Crea practice, and I did. But how could the word *practice* convey my understanding of the psychological level of Ganesh Baba's teachings?

Chitta is the field of the psychic apparatus. It is the overt expression of Cosmic Consciousness on a slightly lower key. But its importance in the scheme of our psychic and parapsychic life and particularly its pristine purity and crystal clarity (Chitta-sudhi) is the prime precondition, inter alia, along with a host of others, for any spiritual progression worth the name.

Yes, with an asudha chitta or impure overt consciousness, one may maintain, make hay while the sun shines, and manage to snatch patches of material prosperity, creature comforts, and luxury—a measure of success minus inner peace and repose—a constant prick of conscience and a constant repeating of our ever-repeating violation of human ethics. With moral space weak, one hardly may expect any spiritual progression worth the name. Sound ethics and moral discipline is the bedrock of a balanced life: a life blending happily the spiritual and the secular.

There can be, however, no basis for sound ethics without preliminary purification and refinement, subtilization and sublimation of the medium, or field (chitta) in which the psychic apparatus of man operates. It is evident that the working of the psychic apparatus cannot be as smooth—and trouble-free—with the medium in which it functions, full of sludge and grit, the inertia and grossness of the elemental matter with which the modern, material man is malignantly involved. So the techniques—the ethical principles, the moral formulae of all the religions of the world—have great importance for the proper operation of our psychic apparatus, which is, indeed, under heavy strain and overload due to the lack of due measure of psychic purification.

Like the words *consciousness* and *intelligence,* the word *practice* is used here to cover more ground than it does in ordinary English. Practice, P³, indicates conscious action, and Presence, P⁴, receptivity.

Practice is usually thought of as a method of learning that uses repetition. Really, any repeated action or behavior is a practice, for better or for worse. It is my practice to have a cup of tea after dinner, though I know it keeps me from sleeping at times.

Some repeated behaviors are conscious, but most are unconscious. The heartbeat, the breath, the work of our organs and systems, even of the mind, endlessly repeat actions without the interference of the conscious mind. The realm of conscious practice is tiny in comparison. We brush our teeth in the morning, we make the bed, or not, we have a spiritual practice, or we practice an instrument or art, we eat, we work. Even these practices are mostly done unconsciously.

Imagine what the world would be like if we took a serious look at what we pay attention to—if we used the power of attention in a beneficial way instead of letting the light of our consciousness be drawn to whatever is moving in the physical, biological, and psychological worlds, if we refined the psychic field instead of muddying it.

The third phase of Baba's Crea Yoga encompasses the fifth and sixth limbs of Astanga Yoga, *pratyahara,* withdrawal or retraction of the senses, and *dharana,* training the attention and developing one-pointedness.

"ATTENTION IS THE KEY!" he shouted at me once with such intensity that the scene lingers in my mind crystal clear. We were sitting side by side at the kitchen table in our Ovid house in the early 1980s, clear skies peeking through frosty windows, woodstove burning at our backs. I wrote the words in capital letters on my yellow legal pad.

Attention *is* the key. What we pay attention to flourishes. If you pay attention to a houseplant, noticing when it is dry and watering it, its leaves get shiny, and it grows. As every parent, teacher, and manager learns, attention, positive or negative, shapes behavior. Attention is the focusing mechanism through which consciousness flows.

The constant practice recommended for the third level of Crea Sadhana is conscious action. This is the heart of practice: using your free will, your attention, consciously, to the greatest benefit of all.

I like to think of the four levels of Crea Sadhana as four worlds: the physical, the biological, the psychological, and the spiritual worlds. The physical, from one point of view, consists of the material framework on which the subtle hangs, and from another, as the darkest portion of the spectrum, the literal, the stuff, the matter (what's the matter?), the *mater,* the mother. The Western scientific perspective denies that there is anything of the spirit in the physical at all. We don't recognize the nonliteral, the metaphoric, and the symbolic aspects of the material world as part of its realness. In the East everything is spirit, but the physical is still considered its lowest form. As the forefront of the brain, the cerebral cortex, evolved its capacity for abstraction, the physical and its metaphoric cousins, the dark and the feminine, were devalued. Thus, women and dark-skinned people have been maligned by cultures all over the world.

The tantric perspective, however, has always divinized the feminine, physically, biologically, psychologically/mythologically, and spiritually, through worship of the Divine Mother in her infinite aspects.

Indian cosmology has it that we are coming out of a long period when the earth was far from the center of the universe. Sri Yukteswar (1855–1936), Yogananda's guru and Ganesh Baba's uncle by lineage, writes about the yugas, or ages, in *The Holy Science.* With a few minor differences in calculation, the ancient Indian calendar coincides with the Mayan calendar. Astronomy confirms that the earth is moving closer to the intense radio source named Sagittarius A*, thought to mark the center of the Milky Way, which has recently been confirmed to be a supermassive black hole. The theory of the yugas says that as the earth moves closer to that center, human understanding grows subtler and subtler. Baba used the examples of our new understanding and use of electricity, unknown only a couple of centuries ago, and now electronics. The subtleties of consciousness are still beyond us, but refining the power of attention and imbuing whatever you do with relaxed, alert consciousness is possible. Pay attention to what you pay attention to; stay present; lead a conscious life. Every moment becomes spiritual practice when you interact with whatever life presents (P³) in a state of relaxed, alert awareness (P⁴).

With practice, the mind learns not to wander in time or space but to stay still and focused. Like the other two all-the-time practices, keeping the back straight and the breath deep, giving full attention to the present is easy to do but hard to maintain. The benefits of taking responsibility for what you pay attention to, to adopting "conscious action" as a practice, are numerous and profound.

Baba recommended specific visualization exercises to train the attention. Like all the practices he recommends, pinealization is a scientific, spare, and systematic route to the goal.

Keith Lowenstein who knew, loved, and traveled with Baba during the same years I knew him, and who became a physician at Baba's suggestion, describes the exercises and how they affect the body and mind.

Keith Lowenstein

The exercises discussed so far are techniques that can change the organization and sensitivity of our central nervous system, including our brain. It is our ability to work that system in new and different ways that transforms our reactions to, and experience of, the environments that surround us. The sections above speak of the basics of proper posture and breath. Both those exercises are, in and of themselves, examples of simple, yet elegant attention-training techniques. Retracting our outwardly focused senses within (as explained below in descriptions of P³ and P⁴) further challenges our brain to work within itself in new ways. Whenever we learn something new, our neuronal connections change. This happens at extraordinary rates of a million changes per second. Technically speaking, this is called neuroplasticity, more commonly known as learning. We are living in a time when there is a need for more citizens of the planet to learn and practice these techniques of inner transformation.

Although we think of our brain as one organ, it is really a compilation of different systems that have evolved a language through which they can communicate with each other. These various parts have evolved to serve various functions in various animals over the course of evolution. Within our brain these parts are now an interdependent group, with each part maintaining some elements of independent function. This way of looking at the brain is sometimes referred to as the triune brain.

What meditation does is shake up the status quo between these various groups within the brain. Meditation is one among many self-regulatory techniques that brings a different order to the neuronal networks within the central nervous system. It is this new pattern of communication among the networks that allows whole new properties to emerge that were not present, or even predictable, before the new order. That is what the comment "meditation just comes" means. Meditation is the emergence of a new property or experience for that individual's central nervous system.

What is particularly wonderful about the emergent properties of meditation is that the deep, reactive, reptilian survival instincts (that can be reinforced by trauma and fear) are calmed and arrive at a new set-point after a meditative experience. With repeated practice or one particularly strong experience, these neuronal networks achieve long-lasting change. All of a sudden the individual has a different experience of the environment around him or her. Survival of the fittest is replaced by a sense of transcendence and being part of a whole that is greater than one's self. The tenacious human urges of greed, control, and power are replaced by cooperation, compassion, and patience.

Why does all this matter anyway? The fact is we, as human beings, are no longer a sustainable species. The planet has been conquered, and we are now conquering our own species. Instead of an external focus on the next plane trip to some exotic locale where the trees have been cleared for the hotel, we need to focus on our inner world of neuronal networks.

The vast forests of neuronal networks within are physically changed by all our experiences. If our neurons only know to look outward for satisfaction, greed will remain the focus of our human experience. If our neurons can be coaxed to experience peace and calming within, the neural networks of humanity across the planet will rewire in such a fashion that a new humanity will emerge. As each individual has his or her own meditative experience, that individual's relation to the population as a whole changes. Once the tipping point in the number of humans with these experiences is reached, new global patterns of human interactions will emerge. Our hope is to move forward on this journey of internal neuronal-network rewiring and emerge at a new apex of human evolution.

Once the spine, breath, and attention are aligned—the back is straight, the breath is long, slow, and deep with pauses at the end of the inhale and exhale, the eyes are rolled up and crossed, and the attention focused on the glow of the pineal gland—Baba recommends stopping at each of the chakras and piercing it with the needle of your attention. He calls this exercise "plexii-plucking." The chakras are the subtle analogue of the junctions of nerves along the spine. They don't align precisely with their physical counterparts, but they can be sensed with practice and will reveal themselves slowly. Some people can discern them by the frequency of their vibration, others by color or sound. In Baba's tidy system they follow the pattern of the rainbow and the musical scale. I could feel them before I saw them, and I am just beginning to be able to hear them.

In *Crea Sadhana,* Baba writes:

We have the two optical eyes to "see" physical objects. The "Third Eye" is to see the Effulgent Aura—the basis of our Spiritual Vision of the totality of Knowledge.

When synchronized by concentration at the "point of penetration," the Agyan chakra, Gyral Center, or "Third Eye," Pranayama stimulates the pineal-pituitary complex; indeed, how Complex it is, we common people cannot even guess. But the four Fields do meet at a Common Focus, and when, by concentrated attention, the striver is ultimately able to fix his full mental attention at that spot between the eyebrows, he begins to gain intuitive knowledge of the reality of the so-called non-self, the dream world of 4-d "objects" and "events." The Reality of Unity in Spirit then bursts forth.

Our psychic fixity or attention to the Gyral Center can lead to our release from the relativity of our dreamlike sense perceptions, leading to our experience of super-sensuous intuition and thus awakening our awareness of the Absolute or Spiritual Existence-Consciousness-Bliss: Satchitananda. At the crucial point or "circle" at the third eye, the kutasth, there is a unique opportunity to directly pass into the causal body from the gross without passing through the various intermediate layers of the complex subtle bodies. It provides a safe springboard for diving in to the Divine in man, rousing it, and making it descend into our day-to-day lives, thus fulfilling the spirit of the motto: "spiritualize the secular."

Under Crea-Concentration this pineal-pituitary point glows with incandescent, fluorescent radiation. But before that degree of concentration is reached to enable us to focus our attention at will, the glow is not fully visible in all its glory. This is the intra-optical "gyral glow," which can be seen through appropriate use of the yoni mudra, a digital technique for artificial induction of the Jungian "primordial image." Within that effulgent "light of life" (prana yoti, or bio-psychic corona effect), an "aura of the atman" or the Self may be "seen" as a two-petaled lotus.

This is the "dove" with the dual or twin wings that descended at the time of "baptism with spirit" by Jesus. The twin wings are "insight" and "wisdom." They represent the twin realities of our existence, the reality of body and spirit. They are the two boundaries of the narrow bridge that spans the gap between mind and reality, the gulf between Reality and realization, between actual and potential, between infra- or subconsciousness and ultra- or super-consciousness. Concentration on these infra-optical "primordial images" or "archetypes of the unconscious" rouses or raises the level and then expands the range of consciousness, and ultimately makes for co-existence with Cosmic Consciousness. That, indeed, is the main mechanism of Crea-Cosmification.

The instrument for piercing through the chakras, plexii, or neuro-psychic centers is the needlelike attention, with intelligence as the pinpoint. Pranayama is the propelling power or force, and Kundalini the thread carried through the eye of the needle.

The heads of the nerve cells, which are like tadpoles with a flat head and filament-like tail, are locked or buried into the brain or spinal cord fibers. The nerve fibers are bundled up into nerve trunks. They branch out from the plexii into the extremities of the body. The trunks and the branches between them constitute the nervous system. Its center of activity is the trunk, extending from the brain along the spinal cord to

its tip at the coccyx and the end of the spinal column. It is a
vast communication circuit; complex, complicated, and cute,
much like the system of wires that makes up a telecommuni-
cations network.

Like everything else, the chakras grow and get clearer when the light of attention shines on them. The Theosophists describe exercises like this as building a body of light. In Tantric Yoga it is said that the power of the earth, represented by the coiled serpent Kundalini, and the light of consciousness marry.

On the cosmic level, the breath traveling up and down the spine corresponds to the Breath of Brahma: the long, slow, deep contraction and expansion of the cosmos, pure consciousness, aware of itself, concentrating until it can be sensed, and then becoming subtler and subtler, and more and more complex until it is beyond comprehension; consciousness with seven levels of existence, from the most basic universal patterns (*Pater*) to the most dense matter (*Mater*), and one of essence, for which there are no words.

The subtle spine is like a flute that plays music with color. It sings our state of mind.

> *The world speaks to me in colors.*
> *My soul answers in music.*
>   RABINDRANATH TAGORE

8
PRESENCE
Constant Awareness of Consciousness

> *Whatever we know is a filtered product of our psyche. We cannot conceive what the soul would be like without the psyche; we have no language for it now. We may know it, but we can't transmit it through language.*
>
> From a lecture in New York City, 1982

Meditation is not something you do; meditation comes.

CHRISTIAN PILASTRE

> "Trust no future, howe'er pleasant
> Let the dead past bury its dead
> Act, act in the living present
> Heart within and God overhead"
> — Longfellow.

"Trust no future." Baba loved to quote these lines from Longfellow.

Straight body, straight breath, straight attention, straight awareness of consciousness (remembrance of god).

Undated handwritten notes

It wasn't that my most recent trip to India failed to satisfy my spiritual longings or to supply me with new information for the book, both specific and general. In fact, a group meditation I participated in, led by Mark Dyczkowski in Benares, was extraordinarily inspiring. The meditation took place at dusk in Mark's house right on the ghat, in a room with big windows, wide open to the sounds, sights, and smells of the Ganges.

On the day of the meditation, Roxanne and I took the night train from Bareilly to Benares, arriving before dawn, just in time to take a rickshaw to our guesthouse at Assi Ghat (too late, alas, to see Ganga Math once more); we dropped off our things and headed back out to see the sun rise.

Such a privilege.

Later, we sat in the sun on the wide stone steps, sipping chai and warming our hands on the little rounded clay cups it comes in. Chai wallahs bearing pots of tea and milk, with baskets of cups hanging from yokes made of sticks, wander along the ghats early in the morning, setting up shop wherever there are customers. Our vendor was a formidable man, old but still large, his long beard tucked into sadhu robes, and his massive head of dreadlocks tied up in swaths of fabric. (We didn't know if he was a wise man or a wise businessman, but either way, he played the role well.)

As we finished our chai, we realized that we were sitting just below Mark's house.

No one answered our rings and knocks (it was seven in the morning, after all), but the pandit who tends the small temple that shares the

Mark Dyczkowski's house on the ghat in Benares. The painting over the door is the symbol of the Divine Feminine. (Photo by Eve Neuhaus)

step with Mark's front door came over and showed us that he had a key. He would be glad to wake Mark for us.

Soon we were enjoying a second cup of tea and learning that we had arrived on the very day that, after forty years of study, writing about, and teaching Kashmiri Shaivism as a scholar, and as many as a practitioner, Mark was about to begin teaching Trika Yoga.

So, of course, we came back at dusk. The meditation focused on being aware of our own awareness.

Mark Dyczkowski on Consciousness

Consciousness is the precious door to infinite Being.

If we stop to reflect on the nature of consciousness, we begin to discover its many marvelous qualities. It is a surprising fact that people hardly notice that they are conscious. Surprising, because consciousness is the most fundamental fact of our lives. If we were not conscious, we would not exist. Consciousness is our very existence; it is our Being. It is not being in any particular way, like being happy or sad, male or female; consciousness is just as it is.

If we consider the nature of consciousness, we find consciousness is present in every moment of our lives. It is everywhere we are at all times and in every state, whether we are awake, dreaming, or in deep sleep. Without consciousness we could not experience anything, we could not do anything.

Even so, consciousness is not a "thing." It exists; indeed, it must exist. If it were not to exist, nothing we experience in any way could have any existence for us. Yet consciousness is not something among other things. Consciousness is not finite. This is a wonderful fact. If we experience consciousness as it is in itself—just consciousness—we experience infinite Being. Indeed, the fact that we are conscious means that we experience infinite Being all the time.

Once we understand that, a little more reflection reveals another astonishing fact. Nothing we experience is outside consciousness. Everything appears within it, as reflections do within a mirror. Great or small, distant or nearby, things appear just as they are in the mirror, without changing it in any way even though they are within the mirror and, in a way, a part of it without being a piece of it. So consciousness is not only present everywhere at all times, but also, due to its existence, everything else we experience exists in the way we experience it.

It is a tremendous loss that we don't pay attention to this fundamental fact of our lives. Although we don't lose any "thing," we lose everything.

If you don't believe me, try it for yourself. Pay attention to your consciousness. Experience it. Don't just look at the reflections in the mirror; see the mirror also. You can try this as you sit quietly alone or in the midst of your daily activity. If you give yourself a chance to experience consciousness, to be aware of it, you will begin to see life differently. Soon you will find out for yourself that consciousness inspires us with the wisdom of inner insight.

You will discover that consciousness is the infinite living Being people have prayed to for millennia as God.

And even more wonderful is the discovery that this is who you really are.

As these things go, I must have been ripe for the teaching. I was thrilled with the shift in my perspective that came about during the meditation, and I found I was able to return to the experience easily during daily life afterward. Being aware that I was aware added an exciting dimension to life, and I could do it any time I remembered to.

Back home in California, I began my morning and evening Crea practice and set to work writing the commentary on the transcript. When I found it hard to find the flow of writing, I thought I would give in to the call of the spring garden for a short time. I found Mark's lectures on the Tantrasara online, downloaded them onto my iPod, and focused my attention on being aware that I was aware as I weeded and planted.

At about the same time, Eckhart Tolle was on Oprah Winfrey's TV show, and his teachings suddenly reached a vast audience. Tolle's message about Presence aligned with Mark's. Using the Cycle of Synthesis as a model, I could see how being present in the sense that Tolle and Mark talked about raised consciousness from the level of Mind to the level of Intelligence. So Presence required leaving the thinking mind behind. Working in the garden or cleaning the house, I found I could maintain a sense of being aware that I was aware while paying full attention to the task at hand. It was easy to be present, and Presence was full of joy.

Soon I was so engaged in the practice of being present that I lost interest in my regular practice entirely. I kept my back straight out of habit more than commitment and worked on watching my breath rather than controlling it. Crea's step-by-step process, aimed at an end I never reached, paled in the face of the glory of the present moment. Baba's elegant Indian English took on an old-fashioned and stodgy sound even though I recognized the gems hidden in it.

For several weeks I set the manuscript and my Crea practice aside, and I gardened and cleaned the house instead. I wanted to be completely out of my head. I stopped listening to lectures on my iPod and threw myself into the present as fully as I could.

I knew that eventually I had to go back to my Crea practice (I had a contract for this book, after all), but the moment persisted in calling me to the garden. Time passed, more than the couple weeks I had allotted.

Meanwhile, my relationships with my family, pets, and neighbors blossomed, and friends commented that there was a new light behind my eyes. My eating habits changed. I lost weight. My house and garden glowed, as anything getting that much attention will. Tolle's system is very forgiving—I stopped scolding myself for not doing this or that, trying instead to do my best at whatever was in front of me. Tolle's teaching trains you to be receptive, openhearted, and nonjudgmental. When you give up resistance, life flows along easily.

Periodically I would try Crea again, but it wasn't the same. The exercises I had been doing for so many years were lifeless in comparison to the simple joy of going through life in this new awakened state.

Then, one day as I transplanted some lilies, I had a marvelous "Aha!" It struck me that time really *is* an illusion. Baba taught us that time is an illusion, and even before I met him I was convinced of the artificiality of time systems, but it wasn't until I stood there at that moment, patting the soil around the lilies, that I really got it. My perspective changed dramatically. I'm free, I thought! I'm no longer tied to yesterday or tomorrow! The realization instantly released me from the need to worry about my in-laws coming next week and from a lifetime of regrets and resentments. And, miraculously, the moment I stopped believing in time, I found I had all the time in the world.

> Consider the lilies of the field, how they grow; they neither toil nor
> spin, yet I tell you, even Solomon in all his glory was not arrayed like
> one of these. (Matt. 6:28–29)

This euphoria lasted a few days. A couple of friends were experiencing a similar shift at the same time; it wasn't until we got together that the downside of our new perspective surfaced. We'd all missed appointments. That's what happens when you leave time behind completely.

It occurred to me then that the concentrative practices of Crea would probably correct the imbalance, but it was another week or two before circumstance and my conscience got together and woke me up early enough in the morning and inspired enough to return to my Crea practice. Finally, obstacles removed, I began stretching one morning, and the synthesis I had sought was obvious.

Tolle's practice of Presence is a *being* practice. The first three Ps of Crea Yoga are *doing* practices. (*Kriya*, after all, is Sanskrit for "action.") It seems painfully obvious now, but it hadn't occurred to me until then that I could be present while practicing Crea. This alert, awake awareness, even though in talking or writing about the fourth P, Baba repeatedly speaks of and urges his students to maintain it at all times.

Baba's language is different, but here he's talking about what Tolle sometimes refers to as Presence, space consciousness, or stillness:

Pronov is the tonal notation denoting the primal vibration of the initial polarization of the pre-creative Unitary integral field and its subsequent sequential diversification or differentiation into the present state of the manifold Cosmos in which we are uniquely involved as creatures and occupiers.

Eckhart Tolle's teaching is mostly about the interface between mind, intelligence, and consciousness on Baba's chart. He suggests that if you change your relationship from resistance to acceptance of what *is* (the bottom half of the chart), you will allow pure consciousness to flow into daily life, spiritualize the secular, discover the sacred in the commonplace.

Tolle recommends various "portals" opening the mind to the divine intelligence and consciousness: paying full attention to the present, feeling the inner body, conscious breathing, and more.

> *You are living in an extra-cerebral rut—come into the cerebral, the here and now, this here-and-now-going-going-gone world!*
>
> "The Rochester Raps," recorded by Ira Landgarten

Ganesh Baba recommends one prime portal: continuous wordless repetition of the sacred syllable OM.

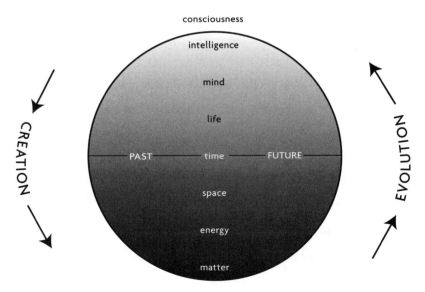

The Cycle of Synthesis with still another emphasis

Pronov-mentation—P⁴

Pronov is the Primordial Pulsation of Cosmic Consciousness, the primal vibration of the Unconditioned Ever-existent Absolute: the Brahma Maha Sunya in its prime creative movement. It is said to be the seed syllable of all scriptures, the sacred and secret phonetic notation of all esoteric teachings. Indeed, it is the Prime Creative Cosmic Vibration, the very first "Word."

Remember the first sentence of the Book of John in the Bible: "In the beginning was the Word, and the Word was with God, and the Word was God." Also remember the initial epigram in the Gita, "Om"; and Alif Laam Meem from the Quran. Remember also the opening epigram of Buddha's personal incantation, OM NAMO BHAGAVATE ARHATYE BUDDHAYA SAMYAK SAMBUDDHAYA. They are, indeed, the highest common syllables in all the exoteric and esoteric revealed religions of the world. OM, AUM, HUM, AMEN, AMEEN, I AM, HONG-SAU, are all variations of that Primal Sound, the Sabdha Brahma, resonating in us as the propeller of the Cosmic Dynamics, making us move about on the stage of the Cosmic drama of Creation (-) and Evolution (+) of Prakriti and Purush. We are indeed puppet-actors of Pronov, the Prime Mover of the Universe.

Mental impinging or plucking the plexii with the repetitive resonance of Pronov (ajapa or non-intoned) and the simultaneous "tuning" of the rhythm of respiration to the rhythm of pronov-mentation reproduces at once the Creative and Evolutionary Vibrations of Universal Cosmic Action or Absolute Pulsation, Infinite to Infinity via the finite.

By appropriate Crea-control of the Cosmic Prime Mover, inset at our Kutasth or Christ Center, we can bring together the primary, or first, fusion of the body, breath (life), and brain (mind) into a single complex called b^3, or the coordinated "Kutasth-centered Intelligence." Crea is also called Union with U^3-Integral, or Union per Intellect, Buddhi-yoga of the Gita. In the Crea scheme, the Cosmic Octave is represented by the 8 plexii of the spinal column, a replica of the octave of the Creative Process. The life process is prolonged, and psychological evolution is accelerated by the "restful repose" of respiration. Metabolism is enhanced by plexii-plucking. The propulsion of pranic currents and Kundalini energizes the cerebral-spinal centers of the neurovascular network. Proper practice of Pranayama reinforces Pronov with an optimal oxygen supply and moderate muscular modulation. But the main thing is the removal of the plugs blocking the smooth flow of Kundalini through its designed retro-rocket rise through the chakras, which need successive unplugging of the neuro-knots.

Thus, Crea-pranayama, together with nonverbal mentation of Pronov, systematically and scientifically synchronizes the basic functional systems of the organism. It unites brawn, breath, and brain in a single harmonious complex, and that automatically attracts sharp intelligence, which naturally enough tears through the veil of maya—reversed reality.

In its basic action, Crea corrects the conflicts in the harmonious functioning of the basic complex, b^3. The complex alloys easily with the ultra-intellect, or para-buddhi, and eventually forms the "deha-prana-mana-buddhi," for example, the brawn-breath-brain buddhi, or b^4-complex. This complex is then synthesized with the basic-ego-principle and becomes the "brawn-breath-brain-buddhi-basic-ego," or b^5 complex.

When this complex as a harmonious composite synchronous unit is concentratedly focused at the Christ-Center, the ajna chakra, the gyral glow shows up, leading to auto-enlightenment. The b^5 complex melts in the Crea-crucible at the Kutasth, and the aurora borealis of spiritual light, or Cosmic Effulgence, bursts forth in its glittering, gladdening, glaring glory—the "Glory of God" the immanent. That is the b^6 complex, the ultra-Cosmic Consciousness. Next comes the b^7 complex, when the Ego-principle is added, and next comes Reality—the synthesis of Absolute and Absolute Spirit. The Ego-unit, Jeev, awakens in Shiva; the cosmic self "individual" is transformed into the Cosmic "collective."

The immanent "ego," the basic unit of consciousness, the seventh chakra or roof-brain-occipit complex, becomes imperceptibly integrated with the Transcendental and both fuse into Ultimate Reality, perhaps to rest there in Eternity.

Mental ajapa of Pronov, P^t, on the chakras in the ascending and descending order over long, restful, reposed periods of Crea-meditation, without verbalization or movement of vocal cords or tongue or lips, fixes the mind on its natural trajectory to the Everest of auto-evolution, Communion with Cosmic Consciousness. Pronov is the tonal notation denoting the primal vibration of the initial polarization of the precreative Unitary integral field and its subsequent sequential diversification or differentiation into the present state of the manifold Cosmos, in which we are uniquely involved as creatures and occupiers. It is not just an adventitious symbol or arbitrary notation. It represents the natural, existential mode of diversification of the Mono to the Many.

Thus, it is the main creative track to the Absolute. The Crea system utilizes this property of Pronov to accelerate the process of reaching back to the Creative Focus at Infinity and the arrival at the Everest of Evolution.

Coexistence with the Absolute is indeed absolution, or salvation, and is, in effect, the gaining of the "transcendental, integral satchitanand state of consciousness." All religions have their revealed scriptures and their sacred syllables, or Word. Their phonetic or tonal similarity is indeed striking and underwrites the underlying unity of all religions, processes, or routes to reunion with the Absolute, of which Crea emerges as the "Crucial Key"—the master key to synthesis and integration.

It took me all those years, all that more recent daily practice, some time off, and listening to other teachers before a deeper understanding of Pronov came to me. The relaxed, alert awareness I was trying to maintain in the garden *is* the background, the OM, the consciousness, in which the first three Ps of Crea are meant to be practiced.

The first three Ps are masculine in essence, a step-by-step linear progression to a goal, which is the fourth level, the eventual remerging of the self with the Self. Through conscious action, they align and still the body, lengthen and still the breath, and tune the attention to one-pointedness by blocking sense perceptions.

> The light of the body is the eye: if therefore thine eye be single, thy whole body shall be full of light. (Matt. 6:22)

Presence, which Tolle says over and over is *not* a practice but must be expressed as if it were in order for it to be understood at all, requires the mind to relax its focus, to let go, to offer no resistance. It opens the awareness as fully as possible, welcoming sensation, recognizing the present as the Source. It is a more feminine practice.

Since then, my Crea practice has been at a whole new level. I do each exercise as if it was not a means to an end. I give each move, each breath, each visualization, each mantra, my full attention. I recognize and lightly dismiss thoughts of what I should be doing and let the process take over. Quality takes precedence over quantity. Oh, my.

The shift in consciousness that Baba, Eckhart Tolle, Mark Dyczkowski, and many others are talking about *is* happening now. Conscious awareness is growing, whether you buy into the idea or not. It's another manifestation, a huge one, of the rise of the feminine that Jung predicted so many years ago. The trick, for me at least, was to move into the new consciousness without forgetting the schedule.

	P¹ POSTURE	P² PRANA	P³ PRACTICE	P⁴ PRESENCE	
	PHYSICAL	**BIOLOGICAL**	**PSYCHOLOGICAL**	**SPIRITUAL**	
always	straight back	long, slow, deep breathing and good diet	full attention on the present	no resistance— letting go	**PHYSICAL**
dawn & dusk	asana: stretching and limb-limbering	pranayama: jet breath & deep breathing with and without retention	pinealization: eyes rolled up and crossed	mantra: ceaseless silent repetition of OM or other sacred sound	
always	good posture improves breathing	good diet and deep breathing improves mental state	deep breath centers, controls mood and pain	relaxed alert awareness	**BIOLOGICAL**
dawn & dusk	breathing with asana	pranayama exercises	concentration exercises: one-pointedness	relaxed, reposed rhythmic breath	
always	conscious posture & movement	conscious breathing & eating	conscious action	constant awareness of consciousness	**PSYCHOLOGICAL**
dawn & dusk	attention exercises	breath/chakra exercises	visualization exercises: light	meditation: receptivity	
always	being present	being present	being present	ॐ	**SPIRITUAL**
dawn & dusk					

Baba's 4 Ps revisioned

The progressive spirit draws upon its heritage or lessons of the past. I propose to forge ahead into the future with the dynamic spirit of progressive perfection of the present. The present is only a moment, a temporary pause in the procession of the past into the future. This is the march of eternity in its infinite cycles of cyclic exchange.

$$\text{u}^4\text{-Integral} = +\int_{dm.}^{\infty}$$

$$\text{u}^4\text{-Integral} = \infty\infty^{\infty} \cdots$$

The present may be perceived as the significant nodes in these cyclic exchanges. The Cosmos is in balance due to the delicate balancing action of the cosmic cyclic exchange between the prime polarities of the Ultimate Universal Unity—an inconceivable "Infinity" and "Eternity" rolled into "one"!

For us all, it is a uniform progression of a procession of presents—moments in time in a precession of events, our physical empirical space-time Cosmos as conceived by Einstein.

Indeed, our journey is from Infinity to Infinity via the finite temporal universe. Infinity is our origin and also our grand goal. We are like "cosmonauts" catapulted from Infinity into this finite 8-dimensional 8-categoried conventional cosmos.

It is our first job, perhaps the only important one, to maintain the machine—this space capsule—in its optimal operational order: O^3. It is not only physical, not only biological, not only psychological, not even totally spiritual, but optimalization of all phases of our being—simultaneously and synchronously—for achieving optimal evolution along with *optimal creativity. The synthesis of creativity with evolution alone can click the cosmic gears to enable us to go back to our launching station at Infinity.*

We have not only therefore to plan or work for "here and now" but also for "then and there." "Here and now" is our finite, limited phase—a short sojourn on this planet earth. "Then and there" is our permanent address in the past (prenatal) and the future (postmortal). In between is our so-called here and now, which has gone back to the limbo of the past, and the moment, "here and now," which has shifted and slipped into what was the future "then and there."

So our real course is from "then and there" to "then and there" via "here and now."

I finally realized that I had to teach the new version of Crea with the new words before I felt comfortable changing Baba's language. It was only after a period of experimenting with teaching the four Ps in their new form that the deeper understanding and the words began to flow.

In *Sadhana,* Baba quotes Swami Vivekananda:

At last dawns the full blaze of light in which the little self is SEEN to have become ONE WITH THE INFINITE. Man himself is transfigured in the presence of this "Light of Love" [the Kutasth, seen at Crea initiation or during lucky psychedelic experiences] and he or she realizes at last that beautiful and inspiring truth—that LOVE, the LOVER, and the BELOVED are ONE.

9

COSMO-NUMEROLOGY

During the first few days I spent with Baba, he hammered cosmo-numerology into me. The powerful experience of recognition propelled by equally powerful joints and Ganesh Baba's singular intensity blew away any preconceptions I'd had. Gone, too, was any resistance. Gone, as well, are my notes from those days, but I got the message.

My mind was open. I was alert, awake, and aware; at Baba's continuous request, I was holding my back straight and breathing properly—"Breathe!" he'd shout at me in the middle of a sentence as he explained how one becomes two, two three, three four, four eight, and eight, ad infinitum.

Baba's teaching was succinct, and I was too much in awe to ask many questions, so he spent most of our time together repeating the basic sequence of his cosmo-numerology to me in different ways and contexts.

"Consciousness is One. When it becomes aware of itself, there are two. The two interact, and then there are three. Two self-powers into four and, by interacting with three, becomes eight, and eight multiplies ad infinitum!"

Numero-Cosmological Basis of Cosmo-Com

"Crea" can be conceived as the first cause or the "act" of creation, and perhaps the last Act of Evolution. It is also the "Cause" of its continuance or sustenance and of its cessation or dissolution. That which is true of the Cosmos is also true of Man, the "mean" between the macro- and the microcosm.

Prior to this primal "ACT" there was no action. There existed an Absolute Existence, an Eternal Consciousness, and an unbroken Bliss, Sat Chit Ananda; beyond any term of dual description, such as manifest/unmanifest, positive/negative, there is Neutral.

Let us now try to follow step-by-step the course of creation.

Polarization of one (Neutral) into two, for example (Prime Polarity)—a couple of Creation: Purush, Spirit (+ve), and Prakriti, Nature (-ve);

The two polarities (Points—vindu) interacted, giving rise to Three, the Prime Triplicity, the 3-phased propagatory principle (Trigunas);

The same interaction produced Prime Notal Vibration: "Pronov" (Nada)—A, U, M;

Next, the two polarities became self-powered: $2^2 = 4$ (quaternary);

Then 2 and 3 interacted, by cubing of the couple $2^3 = 8$ (octave);

And then creation continues on and on by "doubling" of the "Octave" thus:

23 —24 —25 ...2n...........infinity.

Thus it can be clearly conceived that the Prime Principle

(The One Absolute Brahma) is beyond Polarity (Vindu), Vibration (Nada), and Calculus (Kala).

All these acts happened within the Prime Principle, the Continuum of Cosmic Consciousness, which is present in every number, integer, or fraction as an inherent factor: 1 (one). Thus, $1 = 1 \times 1$; $2 = 1 \times 2$; $3 = 1 \times 3 \ldots$ and so on. And these Primal Creative Acts have given rise to the Primal quaternary: by self-powering of the Prime Polarity: $2^2 = 4$ and the Prime Octave: $2^3 = 8$.

Attainment or realization of this Prime Principle is the prize, or ultimate aim, of any kind of yoga. Happily for us, the Prime Principle is inherent in every item of creation. We human beings have to evolve first psychologically and then spiritually to be in tune with that. It is our specific course of evolution; our life as a biological being can only be fulfilled in our optimal evolution by being in tune with Cosmic Consciousness.

Crea Sadhana, the practice as Baba taught it, is the most important manifestation of the numerological sequence for humans (he used the word *mankind,* which I think is accurate but carries too much baggage to use here) because it is a direct connection between consciousness and matter through the matter closest to us, the body. Although our understanding of what consciousness and matter are has evolved over time, Ganeshian synthesis is the most direct and all-encompassing synthesis that Baba could come up with, given his particular experiences and influences.

In light of Baba's search for synthesis, Crea seeks balance in all its aspects: nature and spirit; positive, negative, and neutral; the physical, the biological, the psychological, and the spiritual; ad infinitum. His contention is that it is this balance that makes it the most direct route through the body to cosmic consciousness.

From the start, Baba wanted all transactions done in a variation of the number 108, if at all possible. For instance, this book should have 108 pages and cost $10.08. His explanation of the significance of the auspicious number is arithmetic: 108 is 1^1 x 2^2 x 3^3 ("one-to-the-power-one times two-to-the-power-two times three-to-the-power-three" or "one times one times two times two times three times three"). It represents increase, abundance.

Wikipedia and other websites list dozens of significant appearances of 108 in the East and a growing number in the West. There are 108 beads on malas and rosaries, traditional Hindu and Christian prayer beads; and Hindu deities have 108 names. In Homer's Odyssey, Penelope has 108 lovers, and in astrology there are 9 planets and 12 houses ($9 \times 12 = 108$).

The number itself contains a startling number of coinciding mathematical patterns. Among them, 108 is an abundant number: it is smaller than the sum of its divisors: $1 + 2 + 3 + 4 + 6 + 9 + 12 + 18 + 27 + 36 + 54 = 151$. It is also a Harshad number, divisible by the sum of its digits: $1 + 0 + 8 = 9$, $108 \div 9 = 12$. 108 is also divisible by the total number of its divisors (12), so it is a refactorable number. The interior angles of a regular pentagon measure 108 degrees each.

The distance between the earth and sun is 108 times the diameter of the sun.

The distance between the earth and the moon is 108 times the moon's diameter. And the diameter of the sun is 108 times the diameter of the earth.

In ancient times people paid more attention to the qualities represented by numbers than the quantities. The explanation for the power of 108 that has always appealed to me most, expressed in traditional terms, is that 1 stands for God or higher Truth, 0 stands for emptiness or completeness in spiritual practice, and 8 stands for infinity or eternity. I see it thus: 1 is about alignment, 0 stands for the whole or nothing, and 8 is for multiplicity and infinity. The numerals are hidden in the mandala at the front of this book.

The mandala is a variation of the Cycle of Synthesis that I use as an illustration of Baba's cosmo-numerology. Embedded in the design, which showed up as a crop circle in England in 2001, is the numeric sequence of creation in geometric form: the largest circle contains two smaller circles of equal size. The perimeter of the two smaller circles equals the perimeter of the larger circle. As the division continues, the relationship does not change. The two smaller circles are divided again to make four still smaller circles across the diameter of the largest circle. The sum of the perimeters of these four is equal to the perimeter of the largest circle, and so on.

In archaic language, 108 can be read "Aught, naught, eight." Aught means *in any degree; at all; in any respect,* naught means *nothing,* and eight means *many.* Thus, 108 contains any, none, and all.

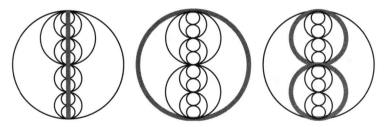

The numerals 1, 0, and 8 embedded in
a version of the Cycle of Synthesis

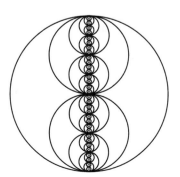

The full mandala

10

ΨΔ

Once a Psychedelic, Always a Psychedelic

When I find myself in times of trouble, Mother Mary
comes to me,
speaking words of wisdom, let it be . . .
"LET IT BE" BY JOHN LENNON AND PAUL MCCARTNEY

> *Live high and die high!*
>
> Often-repeated Ganesh Baba aphorism
>
> *We cannot deny that our origins are in the plant world.*
>
> "The Rochester Raps," recorded by Ira Landgarten

Ganesh Baba had no reservations about crediting the psychedelic movement with the opening of the Western mind to ideas from the East.
He was thrilled to be in *High Times* in December 1982 and referred to
himself as the Highest Hipster. He sang wild and sentimental hymns to
Mother Mary, or Mari-juana, or Mary/John—Mary as mother or Earth,
and Juana (John) as man—and delighted in Timothy Leary's call to
"Turn on, tune in, and drop out."

And, of course, he was great fun to be with, laughing uproariously and dancing and singing for hours on end. There were times when he seemed to need no sleep at all for days and days (and then days when he did nothing but sleep), and there are countless stories about the outrageous amounts of psychedelic substances he could ingest without seeming any higher than usual.

Yet he had no patience for people who took drugs without trying to maintain a straight back or breathing properly, and he told us again and again that it was only necessary to get really high, to take LSD, for example, once. "Once a psychedelic, always a psychedelic."

Smoking ganja with Ganesh Baba was always about going deeper. We often meditated together when we were very high. Rather than letting us relax into a sleep state, Baba expected us to sit up straight, breathe consciously, and *work* our brains.

I remember one morning I arrived early at Roxanne and Jayant's apartment above the New Delhi café in Geneva, New York. I came to write some letters for Baba, a job he gave me periodically, although perhaps a year had passed since I'd last done it in that setting.

We had some tea first, and then a joint or two. At that point I was happy to listen to whatever Baba had to tell me, but he remembered the letters.

"We haven't heard back from Patrick Menicuci!" he announced. "Did you mail the letter?" The letter to Patrick was the last one we'd written sitting at that table.

"A long time ago," I answered.

"But he hasn't answered. Are you sure you mailed it?" I thought I was sure, but marijuana plays with memory.

Baba had me search through his files, but neither the original letter nor a copy (we often made carbon copies of letters in those days) could be found.

We smoked another joint.

"So, you must now remember what we wrote," he told me.

I remember how the anxiety rose from my stomach to my chest. "I can't do that," I said, trying to keep my voice from shaking. "Not in this state."

Baba showed no sympathy. "Sit up straight. Shoulders up and back and down." I could feel my center of gravity shift into my spinal column. "Now breathe with me."

We breathed together, long and loud, slow and deep, until the panic subsided.

"Now, picture the letter. We were sitting right here. It will come."

I sank into the memory: Jayant rolling the joints and serving us tea, the breeze on the curtains, the pen in my hand, Baba's voice dictating. And then I could see it: the blue aerogram lying on the table, the carefully drawn OM at the top, my own handwriting, "My dear Patrick . . ."

I read the letter aloud to Baba.

"Ah cha," he said. "Very good. Now we will write him another."

Somehow, that experience changed my relationship with marijuana forever. Rather than becoming unfocused when I was high, I became focused. Whether it was Baba's presence or my own mental work or some combination of the two, it seemed as if new pathways were carved into my brain that day.

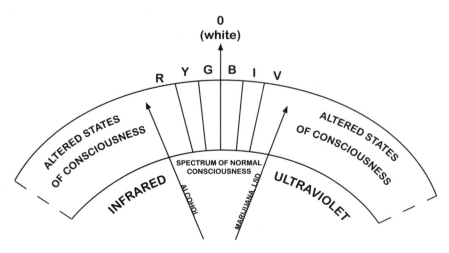

*Spectrum of Consciousness from notes taken at a lecture
by Ganesh Baba in 1980*

> *The world will divide between the alpha-betas and psi-deltas*
> *(alcoholic beefeaters and psychedelics), you will see.*
>
> WBAI interview

We psychedelics must become more familiar with the essence and structure of consciousness, because it is out of consciousness we come and to consciousness we return.

Ganja is gyana yoga—it is an abstraction; you are a little bit abstracted from sensory experience. It gives you room to move your psyche about.

The broad eight categories all operate within the human psyche, but the physical body operates only in the first three dimensions: matter, energy, and space. The fourth dimension, time, we can conceive, but it is like a baby in the womb trying to understand the outside world.

Since time immemorial we have used plant substances to help us recognize the higher frequencies of knowledge.

Corinne Vandewalle remembers some psychedelic moments with Baba

During the winter of 1976–77, my English husband, Henry Shepherd-Cross, our baby daughter, Crystal, and I traveled with Ganesh Baba for about three months. We lived with him in Kathmandu, where he introduced us to his American disciple, Roxanne Kamayani Gupta, and Kapil, her little boy.

Later we flew from Nepal to India, and spent eleven days in police custody: Ganesh Baba, Henry, Roxanne, the two babies, Kapil and Crystal, and myself!!! Just because some paranoid customs man at the border thought we were spies!!! SPIES!!!

After less than a week in the Patna police department, all of the policemen had become Baba's disciples, keeping their backs straight, breathing, and . . . buying bhang-ladous or preparing bhang lassi for Baba and the whole company.

I remember one night the chief had fallen asleep, leaving the key of our "jail" on his pillow, next to him. Baba picked it and gave it back to him in the morning, laughing so much!

Finally released, we went to visit his Kriya-Guru, Yogacharya Tripura Charan Devasharma, in West Bengal. We then took a train from Calcutta to Allahabad in January 1977 to attend the Khumba Mela.

The Anand Akhara gave Ganesh Baba a place under a huge bridge to settle his "Ganeshean camp." We put up tents, and for days our psychedelic, international camp welcomed more and more Westerners: from Yugoslavia, England, California, New York, France, Australia . . . I remember Ira Cohen walking with a skull under his arm, Fantuzzi, Jasper Newsome, Ludmilla, Chaitenya, and many more. An Indian sadhu was in charge of the food, and Henry managed a lot of the organization of the place: tents, carpets, wood, and so forth.

Baba only asked me to take care of my daughter . . . and of his bhang box: I had to make sure it was never empty, which is a harder task than it seems, because the bhang shop in Allahabad was in town, with very flexible opening hours, and Baba's appetite for psychedelia was quite unpredictable . . . I did my best.

Every evening, people from all over the world would gather there just to listen to his high talks.

One night, a married couple from Australia, doctors both of them, arrived, very politely, in our psychedelic circle. They sat in front of Baba, who welcomed them and started to tell them about Kriya Yoga.

Chillums were passed and the air was filled with his vibes of love and humorous consciousness: a pure Ganeshean glimpse of time.

Then Baba said that meditation led to "orgasmic consciousness."

The lady doctor asked him to repeat.

Baba repeated, "Orgasmic! Orgasmic! You don't know what is orgasm???"

Then he turned to her husband and said, "Your wife does not know what is an orgasm?"

Too much is too much. The doctors promptly left the scene and never came back!

Baba was laughing so much.

His tantric teaching was kicking our arses and hammering our ego nonstop, shredding our beliefs to pieces, with so much LOVE!

Love, Life, Light, and . . . Laughter!

Indigenous cultures around the world have always used entheogens to catch glimpses of higher states. I once heard that, when asked if the use of such artificial aids could bring true enlightenment, a wise man, perhaps it was the Dalai Lama, said "Yes, indeed" to the first seven levels but "Never" to the eighth, the goal.

Are drugs necessary to sadhana? Certainly not. The mind can open through countless natural means. Are they useful? Most spiritual journeys begin with some kind of out-of-the-ordinary psychological experience, a jog into a temporary altered state. For much of my generation, the jog came from our youthful experimentation with marijuana or LSD. A seed is planted during the altered state that grows into the desire for permanent awakening. That's what Baba was talking about when he said, "Once a psychedelic, always a psychedelic."

Baba considered himself the true guru of the psychedelic generation. When someone showed him R. Crumb's drawings of Mr. Natural, he was delighted. "It's me!" he crowed. The crowd he drew was as unconventional and eccentric as he was. It's no wonder an organized following never grew around him. In the 1980s Baba predicted that by the new millennium, the beefy-alcoholics would be dying out and psychedelics would rule the world. Though he may have been wrong about that, the current widespread interest in spirituality and the enormous green movement are both surely descended from seeds planted by the psychedelic generation.

Can drugs continue to be useful along the path of sadhana? Ganesh Baba would say yes, within limits—when the body-mind machine is in optimal operating order, when their potential is understood, and they are used appropriately.

In a 1987 interview in *Psychedelic Monographs,* Baba says:

Psychedelia can be a very great boon but it can also be a great curse, for people who have been slouching and oversexing, it can have a very deleterious effect. The human body is a very fine communication apparatus but if the antenna is bent that communication turns into sour communication. Instead of sweet communication or loving communication it turns into angry communication.

The interview continues:

PM: *Are there specific yogic practices to be used in conjunction with psychedelics?*

GB: *Yah. They are called satkarma—the six karmas, the six functions, you know. The first function is carriage. The second is respiration. The third function is proper eating, drinking, and elimination. The fourth function is proper restfulness and the fifth function is the right concepts. You do not crowd your mind with unnecessary information like this mugging system of education.*

The sixth function is the supremacy of nature; filling your brain with the idea that nature is vaster and more potent than we are. The idea of proper place in the cosmos. This is what they call satkarma and it is completely different from the system for non-psychedelics. Their bathing is different, their food is different, their exercises are different.

Unless those things are done they say not to indulge. This should not be indulged in as an intoxicant.

Though the monks of Baba's order had such different rules for living from their nonpsychedelic counterparts, marijuana and other mind-altering substances are an ordinary and permanent part of our contemporary lives, and there are plenty of rules about not using consciousness-altering substances, but few or none about how to use them.

Ganesh Baba taught his rules about their use clearly and consistently. Only drugs that fell into the psychedelic class were permissible. Hard drugs, cocaine, heroin, amphetamines, any narcotic or depressant, even alcohol—in fact, anything but marijuana, hashish, traditional entheogens like peyote, psilocybin, ayahuasca, and LSD—were considered dangerous. Marijuana and psychedelics are not meant for social use. Preferably, wait until you are more than fifty years old. When smoking or taking any psychedelic, keeping your back straight is absolutely essential. Breathing should be controlled, slow, and deep. Focus your attention when high rather than letting it drift, and use the heightened state of awareness to be more present rather than less.

And while it is true that psychedelics offer a preview of higher awareness, a moment of satori, Crea Sadhana—posture, prana, practice, presence—systematically purifies and opens the nervous system to its full capabilities completely naturally. Eventually the need to alter consciousness artificially falls away. If it doesn't, reflect on why it hasn't.

"It is a razor's edge path—you know Somerset Maugham's book, *The Razor's Edge?*" Baba remarked once. "I could be that Ganesh, I am old enough, you know, but my vows do not permit me to say." And he laughed and laughed and laughed.

Creaway Cosmocom

Since after Aldous Hux.[ley] opened, almost first for a white Westerner, the "Door of Perception," many more have walked through it. It has been an "open sesame" for opening out into the infinity of "spaces" and eternity of "times." Space-time has been transcended. An escape has been found for the miserable millions ground down by a relentless impersonal corporate-establishment monster. A whole new generation of aspiring youth has cropped up with their soaring heights and diabolical dives into dire, distressing depths. An ever-increasing yawning generation gap is gaping at all of us in the face. We are now living in a house severely divided within itself. Our ecological equations have touched explosive limits and are merely awaiting ignition. Black box trails presidents like tails of monkeys, faithfully following him/her.

Must we go on living our blind, suffocating round of daily drudgery and deadened sanity, and worst of all, shattered interpersonal relations, broken homes, damning divorces, and wasted wonderful children, flowers of our "life"?

Let's at least save them by putting our heads together on the Creaway—not the only one, but the shortest.

Remember, there may be [many] routes between two points, but only one is shortest, the straight line—simple geometry.

Come one Come All

Come One and All

We welcome you with open arms!

FROM GANESH BABA'S CREA SADHANA

CREAWAY
COSMOCOM

Since after Ald Hux opened, almost first for a white Westerner the 'Door of Perception' many more have walked through it. It has been an 'open seseme' for opening out into the infinity of 'space' and eternity of times. 'Space-time' has been transcended. An escape has been found for the miserable millions ground down by a relentless impersonal Corporate Establishment moriety. A whole new generation of aspiring youth has cropped up with their soaring heights and diabolical dives into dire, distressing depths. An ever increasing awning generation gap is gaping at all of us in the face. We are now living in a house severely divided within itself. Our ecological equations have touched explosive limits and are merely awaiting ignition. Black box trails the president like tails of monkey, faithfully following

    Must we go on living our blind, suffocating round of daily drudgery and deadened sanity. And worst of all, shattered interpersonal

From Ganesh Baba's notebooks

relations, broken homes, damning divorces and wasted wonderful children, ~~are~~ flowers of our 'life'?

Lets at least save them by putting our heads together on the freeway — not the only one but the shortest, surest and the safest.

Remember, there may be many routes ~~road~~ between two points or places but only one shortest; the straight line — simple geometry!

Come one Come all

Come One and all

We Welcome you with open arms

Appendix 1
PRINCIPLES
OF SCIENTIFIC
SPIRITUALIZATION

In August 1968, David Stuart Ryan copied the synopsis of *Sadhana* from Ganesh Baba's notebook, one of the very few things Baba carried in his small bundle of possessions on his return to the Kashmir Valley from a pilgrimage to Amarnath, 15,000 feet up in the Himalayas. A small portion of that synopsis opens the introduction to *The Crazy Wisdom of Ganesh Baba*. The complete synopsis appears here below. The Divine Life Society is Swami Sivananda's organization.

Swami Ganeshanand
Divine Life Society
Darjeeling, West Bengal

Sadhana

The Principles of Scientific Spiritualization
Amplified by Sri Ganesh
Original author: Yogacharya Srimat Tripura Charan Devesharma
Containing the Principles of Cosmic Action or Kriya

We must lose no time in realizing the gravity of our present predicament, as a specific species geared to free will. Though our free will may not be entirely or absolutely free it is also not fettered by any blind, lack-law or lack-love fate. We must realize the gravity of our failure, in our specific property (the gyro-compass of free will), spirituality; and each of us must make it our bounden responsibility to realize our respective shares in the lapse of our species and seek remedy to our individual lapses, which by and large add up to the totality of the general lapse of our species in regard to its most specific property, for example, spirituality.

The next revolution is going to be a spiritual one, and it will have to touch off a chain reaction of personal revolutions leading to total revolution, individual changes leading to a social change. Each of us is responsible for the real revolution in the offing, the revolution of modern man, the modern matter-mad spirit-oblivious man, trying to turn his face toward the spirit, steering an even course between matter and spirit, a harmonious combination of both as complementary aspects of the one Integral Reality. None can conscientiously disclaim his or her responsibility, in which one has to kill nothing but his or her own vices, including lack of spirit or failure of faith. If you are not doing so you are hindering humanity in its general progress.

It is the progression of individuals like you and us that the general progress of humanity consists of. If we neglect our own personal progression along our natural evolutionary trajectory as human beings, blessed with evolved consciousness, we add resistance to the general progress that each of us so hopefully looks forward to.

Our individual fruition cannot also reach a satisfactory stage of completion unless we contribute our share to the general evolutionary progress by properly practicing our personal part. Thus the cause of this oncoming revolution is going to be personal revolution leading to mass revolution. Scientific spiritualization of the individual will, by chain reaction, leads to the spiritualization of the general. Let us each do our personal part in perfecting our spiritualization, then we may hope for the whole of humanity to turn from its present trends over which we find ourselves often tortured. Let us take the step to spiritualize our individual selves in the scientific way indicated in this book; we may be able to infect others with the same spirit by acting as foci of spiritual induction. Spiritualization, especially scientific spiritualization, like magnetism, is inductive, infectious, and readily affects persons proximate to the spiritualized. Spiritual emanations envelop the whole cosmos. Our individual essay in scientific spiritualization has its effect on Cosmic Spiritual Field. It attracts benign blessings to the Universe along with the attainment of grace and blessings by the aspiring individual.

The Cosmic Action (Kriya) technique of scientific spiritualization makes for Cosmic Welfare (Vishorakalyaan). It is supposed to be the Supreme Sacrifice (Yagyan), the Perfect most Propitiation. Being based on the principle of Cosmic Action it makes use of Cosmic Energy (action must generate or absorb energy), which is inexhaustible, to power the spiritual gyrocompass in man. The first benefit that readily flows from Kriya practice is solution of all power problems in the individual man to start with. It activates appropriate energy in the individual psychosomatic and no power shortage or failure is ever felt. Physically, vitally, mentally, intellectually, and even in the planes of the occult or astral, he or she becomes adequately powered if not always demonstrably powerful. They should never be demonstrative of occult powers; but may demonstrate the process or technique if directed to do so by a proper authority on the subject.

Kriya or Cosmic Action, as its name implies, is an active spiritual technique and not a passive process of proselytization. It does not postulate any passivity or inaction. It is not a cult of escapist nihilism, indeed it is the culture of Cosmic Action, as against the inertia of ignorance; that is the crux of the crucial lay techniques of cosmic communion or communication with Cosmic Consciousness, the summum bonum of Universal Spirit or spirituality, as one may call it. This is the supremely attainable consciousness in our highest cosmic plane. Cosmic Consciousness by Cosmic Action, that in short is the broad formulation behind Kriya-spiritualization process.

We must clearly state as to what we mean by Cosmic. It is evidently adjectival of the wind. "Cosmos," which means neither a perfect chorus nor a perfect chaos, but a Cosmos, a medley characteristic of both. The word cosmic has been used in the same spirit and context as Cosmic Rays, the source of which ultra-terrestrial radiations is empirically unknown. But here the scope of the name acquires a broader perspective. The realization of cosmic consciousness as consummation of Kriya practice is, however, not outside the scope of the empirical. It can be as empirically experienced as the observations through the telescope or microscope or spectroscope. The Kriya technique utilizes the eyepiece provided at the pineal plexus within the human cerebrum, along the cerebrospinal channel. The individual ego-consciousness expands the Cosmic Action (Kriya) to embrace the total context of consciousness in the entire cosmos around us—the highest attainable level of consciousness, which the most perfected human beings can ever attain. This is called or rather termed here as Cosmic Consciousness. This is evidently the highest point of spiritualization. That Cosmic Consciousness is the Common, the Highest Common, Spirit in the Cosmos, the Divine Spirit, the Unity that pervades the manifold diversity of the Universe. Realizing that spirit is indeed the essence of spiritualization.

The realization of Universal Unity results in a harmonious rapport being established between the individual and the universal. A sense of belonging, a sense of affinity among all in the Universe wells up in the self-realized soul, making for peace, happiness, bliss, and beatitude. Universal Love acquires a practical significance for the one who has realized the Spiritual Unity of the Universe. This is the real result of spiritualization, the most essential result, the most desirable indeed. This counterpoises the damning nemesis of mad materialism, naked unabashed matter-grabbing maniacal materialism. This takes away the sting from rabid materialism by removing its poisonous fangs, rapacity, and selfishness: love born only of realization of Universality serves as an antidote to separatist selfishness, exclusive acquisitiveness, and aggressive self-aggrandizement. It makes for selfless service and unselfish sharing of the bounties of life with others.

That indeed is Life Divine.

Appendix 2
GANESHIAN SYNTHESIS

By Corinne Vandewalle
("Karunadevi")

Thousands of books, essays, articles, magazines, millions of pages have been written on yoga. I bow respectfully to all those authors, writers, and journalists who have spread the message of yoga and given to the world precious information.

But as Swami Sivananda used to say: "One ounce of practice is better than a ton of theory." I remember that Anandamayi Ma, the highest saint I ever met, could not read or write . . .

Ganesh Baba himself was a great writer, and many of his disciples all over the world keep in their drawers and closets piles of his handwritten (or typed on a very funky old typewriter!) pages or letters.

Nevertheless, when I try to read between the lines of Baba's manuscripts, I find he always comes back to the essential, the spine of his teachings: Practice Kriya! Practice Kriya! . . . and the rest will follow.

Ganesh Baba loved efficiency. Finally, he condensed the whole of his teachings on Crea (Kriya Yoga) on one single page! (See next page.)

MACROMODULATION

P¹: POSTURE (PHYSICAL)	
Easy seat. Carry your column as a column, not as an arch!	Maintain lumbar concavity
Mahamudra for increasing spinal suppleness and tension-release-flexion of the spine	

P²: PRANAYAMA (BIOLOGICAL)	
Reposed rhythmical respiration	Integral breathing, for example, working the upper, middle, and lower lung and also the diaphragm
Decarbonization and oxygenation	

P³: PINEALIZATION (PSYCHOLOGICAL)	
Peering into the pineal	Cross-beaming by intraoptical gazing at the gyral center between the eyebrows
Yoni mudra: genetic modulation (esoteric)	Optical system
Auditory system	

P⁴: PRONOV-MENTATION (SPIRITUAL)	
Primordial notal vibration	Nonintoned, nonverbal, mental repetition of a sacred syllable or monosyllabic mantra such as:
	Aᴜᴍ -Cosmic Creative Sound
	Ethnic modifications of Aᴜᴍ:
	Oᴍ - Aryan
	Rᴀᴍ - Hindu
	Oᴍ, Hᴜᴍ - Buddhist
	Oᴍᴇɴ - Hebrew
	Aᴍᴇɴ - Christian
	Aᴍɪɴ - Islam
	Sᴀᴛɴᴀᴍ - Sikh

MICROMODULATION

P⁵: SYNCHRONIZATION OF THE 4 PS BY SIMULTANEOUS PRACTICE OF THE 4 PS

P⁶: PENCILING (FOCUSING) OF SYNCHRONIZED ATTENTION
Yoni mudra—genetic gesture

P⁷: PLEXII-PIERCING BY PLEXII-PLUCKING

P⁸: PALATAL: KETCHARI-MUDRA (ESOTERIC)

GLOSSARY

Note from the author: My instinct was not to have a glossary at the end of this book. Glossaries tend to fix meaning and limit the potential of words. Nonetheless, as I was writing, I kept this glossary to help clarify my own understanding, and by the grace of Ganesh, it ended up here. Some of the following definitions are taken from Baba's own writing. The rest come from a variety of sources, many without citations. My thanks go to their authors.

abhava: Want or poverty; lack of conformity with one's true nature.

ajapa: The practice of *japa* without the mental effort normally needed to repeat the mantra. In other words, it has begun to come naturally, turning into a constant awareness. The practice of constant remembrance evolves in stages and requires great concentration and practice.

akhara: Akhara means literally the place for practice (the Greek word *academy* has similar meaning) for the protection of Sanatana Dharma. Akhara is divided into eight davas (divisions) and fifty-two marhis (centers). Each Marhi is governed by a Mahant. The top administrative body of the Akhara is Shree Panch (the body of five), representing Brahma, Vishnu, Shiva, Shakti, and Ganesha. It is elected on every Kumbh Mela, and the body holds its post for four years.

Akharas are divided into different types according to the concept of God they worship. Shaiva Akharas for followers of Lord Shiva, Vaishnava or Vairagi Akhara for followers of Lord Vishnu, and Kalpwasis for followers of Lord Brahma.

In the beginning Adi Shankaracharya established seven Akharas namely Mahanirvani, Niranjani, Juna, Atal, Avahan, Agni, and Anand Akhara. Today there are three major akharas (Mahanirvani, Niranjani, Juna) and three minor akharas (Atal affiliated with Mahanirvani, Anand affiliated with Niranjani, Avahan affiliated with Juna). Furthermore there is one small Brahmachari Akhara named Agni, affiliated with Juna.

Akharas were established by Shree Adi Shankaracharya who divided Sannyasa into two categories:

- Astradharis (weapon holders)
- Shastradharis (scripture holders)

The first group is known as Naga Sannyasis; their initiation ceremony takes place only during Kumbh Mela. Only those who were initiated during Kumbh Mela in Prayag are eligible to be Shree Mahants. The initiation ceremony for nagas is different from those for the second group (Paramahansas and Dandis).

The biggest akhara—regarding the number of the Sadhus in it—is Juna, then Niranjani, and then Mahanirvani. The first person in the akhara is the Acharya Mahamandaleshwar, followed by other Mahamandaleshwaras, Mandaleshwaras, and Shree Mahants.

anand (or ananda): Bliss.

atma: The individual soul; the Self, one's spirit.

AUM (or OM): The sound from which all other sounds come, said to have three components, A, U, and M.

biopsychic field: A property of space analogous to but more subtle than an electromagnetic field caused by the motion of life and mind. Also called the psychosomatic field.

Buddhi: [Sanskrit, "intellect"] the higher mental faculty, the instrument of knowledge, discernment, and decision. It contrasts with *manas,* mind, whose province is ordinary consciousness.

Brahma: "To grow" or "to expand" or "to swell." The present state of the True-Stuff of the universe.

chakra: Centers of energy in the subtle body often experienced as wheels and associated with changes in consciousness. Often referred to as connected with the physical body at various locations along the spinal column.

Chitta Vritti Nirodha: Control of the activities of the mind.

Crea-com: Another name for Crea (or Kriya) yoga, short for Crea-communion.

Crea-paravasta: The trans-Crea state, or the state of trans-transaction, Utter

Unity, Cosmic Consciousness; truly living in the here-now, a higher level of Crea initiation.

deha: Body.

effulgence: The state of being bright and radiant; splendor; brilliance.

electromagnetic field: A property of space caused by the motion of an electric charge. A stationary charge will produce only an electric field in the surrounding space. If the charge is moving, a magnetic field is also produced. An electric field can also be produced by a changing magnetic field. The mutual interaction of electric and magnetic fields produces an electromagnetic field.

field: The area affected by a force, its sphere of activity. A magnetic field is the area near enough to a magnet to be affected by its charge.

Four Bodies:

Causal	intello-conscious	spiritual
Subtle	bio-psychic	psychological
Subtle	electromagnetic	biological
Gross	inertio-gravitational	physical

4 Ps: Posture—straight back plus limb-limbering
Pranayama—reposed rhythmic respiration
Pinealization—focused attention on the third eye
Pronov-mentation—mental repetition on the sacred syllable OM

Ganesh: One of the best-known and most worshipped deities in Hinduism. Although he is known by many attributes, Ganesha's elephant head makes him easy to identify. Ganesha is widely worshipped as the Remover of Obstacles, and more generally as Lord of beginnings and the Lord of obstacles (Vighnesha), patron of arts and sciences, and the god of intellect and wisdom. He is honored with affection at the start of any ritual or ceremony and invoked as the "Patron of Letters" at the beginning of any writing.

gross: In esoteric, emanationist, and integral thought, the Gross Realm or Gross Reality constitutes the end link of the chain of emanation. It is usually associated or identified with matter, objective physical reality, and the world of the senses.

Inertio-gravitational field: Einstein found his way to special relativity through the unification of electric and magnetic fields. Electric and magnetic fields are not two separate fields but part of one field, the electromagnetic field. Likewise, space and time are part of one structure, space-time. In the work that led to general relativity,

Einstein made a similar move. According to the equivalence principle space-time and the gravitational field do not exist side by side but are part of one entity, inertio-gravitational field. The unification of the electric and magnetic field led Einstein to the relativity of all uniform motion. For more than a decade he believed that the unification of space-time and gravity would lead to the relativity of arbitrary motion. Around 1920 he realized that this is not true, and he embarked on a new project, the grand unification of electromagnetic and inertio-gravitational fields.

jeev (also *jiva* or *jiiva*): [Sanskrit] Individual soul; ego-unit.

Kantian categories: In German philosopher Immanuel Kant's (1724–1804) philosophy, a category is a pure concept of the understanding.

The idea of categories comes from Aristotle. In John Stuart Mill's explanation, "The Categories, or Predicaments—the former a Greek word, the latter its literal translation in the Latin language—were believed to be an enumeration of all things capable of being named, an enumeration by the summa genera (highest kind), for example, the most extensive classes into which things could be distributed, which, therefore, were so many highest Predicates, one or other of which was supposed capable of being affirmed with truth of every nameable thing whatsoever."

kinesis: [Greek] Aristotelian term for motion or change.

kutasth: "One which is staying steady as an anvil" (Shankaracharya), the glow at gyral plexus or third eye, the *agyan* (or *Ajna*) *chakra,* the point between the eyebrows.

Laksmi: The Hindu goddess of wealth, fortune, love and beauty, the lotus flower, and fertility.

logos: [Greek] Literally, "word," "account," or "reason," the term has a range of meanings in both exoteric and esoteric philosophy from the divine animating principle in things of rational discourse.

maya: The illusion of individuality.

O³: Optimal Operational Order.

ontological: Of or relating to the nature of being.

ом: The sound from which all other sounds come, said to have three components, A, U, and M.

Param: The highest, the supreme.

Paramatman: The Supreme or Oversoul, the Spirit.

plexii (plural of plexus): Points of connection in networks.

prana: [Sanskrit] Life energy. Also called bionic energy.

Pranayama: [Sanskrit] Breath control.

prana yoti (or jyoti): Inner light created by life energy.

Prakriti ("matter"): In the dualistic philosophies of Sankhya and yoga, *Prakriti* is opposed to *purusha* ("spirit"), as the two ontological realities.

principle: A comprehensive and fundamental law, doctrine, or assumption.

Pronov (or pranava): The phonic sound for the sacred symbol OM.

Purusha ("person" or "spirit"): In the dualistic philosophies of Sankhya and yoga, *purusha* is opposed to *prakriti* ("matter"), as the two ontological realities.

Sabda-Brahma: [Sanskrit] Literally, "Word-God"—the Word, "In the beginning was the Word, and the Word was with God, and the Word was God" (John 1).

Sadhak: Practitioner.

Sadhana: [Sanskrit] Spiritual practice.

Sanyal Mahasaya: Shrimat Bhupendranath Sanyal, the renowned yogi and youngest disciple of Lahiri Mahasaya. A householder, highly educated and advanced spiritually, he authored dozens of spiritual books. He established ashrams in Puri, Orissa, and Bhagalpur, Bihar. Born February 28, 1877. Initiated on June 23, 1893, at Varanasi.

Sanyasin: [Sanskrit] In Hinduism, the fourth stage of life, renunciation.

Saraswati: The Hindu goddess of knowledge, music, and all the creative arts.

Shiva: the aspect of the Supreme Being that continuously dissolves to re-create in the cyclic process of creation, preservation, dissolution, and re-creation of the universe.

Swabhava: Conformity with one's true nature.

Tantra: The ancient occult science of vibratory chemistry, the religion of the Mother Goddess Shakti, from the root meaning "to expand" or "to liberate."

"Tantra is that Asian body of beliefs and practices, which, working from the principle that the universe we experience is nothing other than the concrete manifestation of the divine energy of the Godhead that creates and maintains that universe, seeks to ritually appropriate and channel that energy, within the human microcosm, in creative and emancipatory ways." [David Gordon White]

Tripura Charan Devasharma: Born on May 22, 1906, in a village named Lachipur, under Ghatal sub-Division of West Medinipur, a District in West Bengal (India). The village Lachipur is about 125 km south of Calcutta (now called Kolkata), the capital of West Bengal.

He was the eldest son of Krittibas Harh (Devasharma). Krittibas Harh was a very pious man having high spiritual ideas. He used to devote most of his days in worshipping God and chanting mantras (hymn). He used to read Ramayan and Mahabharat and other religious books and recited from those for the willing listeners, who used to gather in his house every evening. Thus Tripura Charan was brought up in a religious atmosphere. He became a devotee of God from his early childhood and the impulses of God grew into his hunger for eternal knowledge.

Lachipur, being a remote village, had no school to speak of, or any college in the vast locality. Accordingly he could not get any formal education. Following the tradition of ancient Indian educational systems, the little boy was sent by his father to a "toll" (a residential Sanskrit School where Sanskrit was taught by a teacher called a pundit) in Radhanagar, a village at a distance of 8 km from Lachipur. The boy had to stay at the pundit's house. After completing his education, he went to another toll in the village of Narajol to get higher education in Sanskrit. During the time of his final examination for a degree in Sanskrit at the University of Calcutta, his father fell ill. Tripura Charanji gave up his studies and plunged into nursing his father. Upon his father's death, he had to maintain a big family left by his father. They had some paddy fields and some cows, which were the main source of income of the family. He used to go to distant fields to tend cows. With his own hand he cut grasses for the cows and carried it to the house holding it on his head. Apart from his family duties, the spiritual questions, which he nourished from boyhood, waved his mind. He asked his father—What is life? From where did we come? Where do we go after death? What is the purpose of such coming and going? His father did not answer him but assured him that in due time he would get the answers from "Sat-Guru."

After his father's death those eternal questions made him restless and sleepless. He moved from place to place, Ashram to Ashram in search of a "Sat-Guru." But how to identify the "Sat-Guru"?

At last the moment came when he got the "darsan" of Yogacharya Satchidananda

Maharaj popularly known as Motilal Thakur and came to know who is "Sat-Guru." He got all the answers of his eternal queries before putting any question to his Lord. He got the initiation from Sri Sri Satchidananda, the disciple of Swami Yukteswar Giri Maharaj. Yukteswar Giri Maharaj was the direct disciple of Yogiraj Sri Sri Shyamacharan Lahiri, the name needs no reference.

In this way Yogacharya Tripura Charan Devasharma got Kriya Yoga Diksha. Thenafter for some years he stayed with his Gurudev at "Chatra Sri Guru Ashram" at Srirampur, another place in Hoghly District in West Bengal. That ashram was also the main ashram of Yukteswar Giriji Maharaj. There his Sadhana began and within a short period he crossed all the stages of "Kriya Yoga" and became "Acharya." He had and still has thousands and thousands of disciples and a good number of ashrams in West Bengal. His main ashram is at Lachipur. The ashram was founded by his Gurudev Satchidananda Maharaj.

In time Yogacharya Tripura Charan became a great Kriya yogi and guru. One of his very famous disciple was Swami Ganeshananda, the Ganesh Baba. Ganeshananda received third Kriya from Yogacharya Tripura Charan.

He gave Kriya Yoga to any person desiring it, irrespective of caste and creed, race or religion. He had some disciples from foreign countries also who used to speak English and French. Although Tripura Charan received no English education, he faced no difficulty having conversations with them.

Tripura Charan always asked his disciples to do their duties to their family first and at the same time practice Kriya. He always told them to maintain their family and simultaneously maintain their religious life keeping their faith on God through the realization that God is omnipotent and omnipresent.

He has kept his ideas and thinking on some of his religious books, namely "Sadhan Bhajan," "Kriya-Yoga," "Diksha Shiksha," "Atma Parichay," and so forth.

After completion of his work and fulfillment of his mission, he entered into "Maha Samadhi" on February 8, 1982, the auspicious day of Maghi Purnima (the full-moon night of the 10th month "Magha" of the Bengali Calendar).

Anybody interested may contact gurudham@bluebottle.com.

U³: Ultimate Universal Unity—the goal of Crea Yoga.

undulatory: Moving in the manner of waves; resembling the motion of waves, which successively rise or swell and fall; pertaining to a propagated alternating motion, similar to that of waves.

Yoga: "Reunion."

INDEX

Page numbers in *italics* refer to illustrations.